DISGUISES OF THE DEMONIC

DISGUISES OF THE DEMONIC

Contemporary Perspectives on the Power of Evil

Edited by A L A N M. O L S O N

ASSOCIATION PRESS / NEW YORK

DISGUISES OF THE DEMONIC

Copyright © 1975 by Alan M. Olson

Association Press, 291 Broadway, New York, N.Y. 10007

International Standard Book Number: 0–8096–1896–6
Library of Congress Catalog Card Number: 74–31321

Library of Congress Cataloging in Publication Data

Disguises of the demonic.

Some of the essays are based on the Lowell Institute lectures for 1973 at the Boston University School of Theology.
Includes bibliographical references.
1. Devil. 2. Demonology. 3. Good and evil.
I. Olson, Alan M., ed.
BT981.D57   235′.4   74–31321
ISBN 0–8096–1896–6

CONTENTS

5

FOREWORD

If the Devil's clearest stratagem is to convince people that he does not exist, his next most clever trick is to become a celebrity. In neither case, then, will he and all his works be taken seriously. For the person with a rationalistic, empiricist perspective, all talk of the demonic or satanic powers is nonsense, a reversion to primitive superstition. So whatever we call evil in human experience is only the regrettable consequence of faulty breeding, adverse environment, or poor judgment. For everything there is not only a season but a reason. A demonic force is no more needed to explain evil than is a transcendent benign deity to provide warrant for good, according to this view.

With respect to the numberless people whose impressionable, pliant minds are manipulated by movies, magazines and sensational fiction it is just the opposite. When demonism is made the fashion and spiritism a fad, the gullible public pays for the mass media which promote them. But the effect of such an epidemic craze is not to heighten people's concern for truly malevolent and destructive evil. Quite the contrary, it leads to a frivolous preoccupation with secondary, suspect and spurious aspects of demonism. This is just a distraction of attention from what is authentically and seriously menacing to human life. Of what import are alleged ectoplasmic phenomena compared to the uncontrolled inequities of food distribution around the world and the consequent starvation of millions? Or, again, how can the mental energy devoted to considering the supposed possession of a little girl be justified in the absence of responsible concern for this generation's spate of homicide and genocide? The popularization of satanism, demonism and a variety of other devotions to occult powers amounts to a trivialization of concern for evil.

Christian faith in particular, from New Testament times onward, has regarded "sin, death and the devil" as neither fascinating nor trivial. We need not accept the ancient notion that the good God finds his equal match in the evil one; nor is it required by Christian faith that Satan be regarded as a "person." It is enough to accept as mystery the fact that "the prince of this world" and "the powers of darkness" refer to whatever malevolent forces there are in creation which contradict and often nullify the good purposes of God.

The authors of this book are not interested in contributing further literature of a frivolous, titillating style. Of such there is more than enough to satisfy the public's sensate demand. In contrast, these essays are mature efforts to meet the challenges of demonism on a serious level.

This book began to take shape in February of 1973, when the annual Lowell Lectures in Boston University School of Theology were presented by Professor McGill, Professor Florescu, Dr. Karefa-Smart, and Professor Ulanov. The six additional essayists were then engaged by Professor Alan Olson, who perceived what argumentation was needed to make this the coherent book it has become.

> J. ROBERT NELSON, *Dean*
> Boston University School of Theology
> 1974

Alan M. Olson

THE MYTHIC LANGUAGE OF THE DEMONIC: AN INTRODUCTION

"THE DEATH OF SATAN," wrote Wallace Stevens, "was a tragedy for the imagination." [1] This line, to be sure, mirrors a sense of loss for the sensitive poet. It contains nothing, however, that would be apt to arouse a sense of loss in the average person either in 1944, when it was written, or today. Indeed, everyone of good, common sense "knows" that there are no angels, gods, spirits or devils and that such mythic personifications are antique beliefs having nothing to do with "man come of age." While children (at least in some of the more intransigent religious circles) are momentarily exposed to the strange biblical and medieval worlds of gods and devils, such phenomena are in the main regarded as elementary pedagogical devices later to be expunged through exposure to the deeper, moral truths of religion.

Steven's lament, however, is no poetic ruse in the face of simply getting on without the gods; resigned, as it were, to being the technological animals we have become. "How cold the vacancy," he continues, "When the phantoms are gone and the shaken realist/ First sees reality;" [2] "cold" and "vacant" because the loss of a capacity for mythic-symbolic language indicates that the very nature and meaning of human experience has been radically altered through a diminishment over which we have little or no control. What, finally, can one say really about a world that has been stripped of the "figural" stuff upon which the imagination thrives and upon which, at least in Christianity, the "sacramental vision" depends? [3]

Writing at the same time as Stevens, and arriving at a remarkably similar conclusion, Dietrich Bonhoeffer observed that the "linchpin" of Western civilization itself had been removed some-

how, and that with the passing of the expressly religious contextu-
alization of meaning and value that prevailed until only recently,
we were suddenly left quite alone and adrift. Reeling still from this
sense of loss we continue to ask, can there be anything meaningful
and salutary about the demystified and disenchanted world within
which we are and live and presumably have our being? Now, indeed, we begin to discover another level of irony in the famous
statement of Dostoevsky's Ivan that "If God is dead, all things are
permissible." In addition to the moral anarchy implicit to an epoch
devoid of divinely ordained normative standards and mandates,
there is also, in fact, the "death of possibility." While the prospect
of unrestrained permissiveness tends, at first glance, to suggest the
boundless possibility of an open-ended freedom, the opposite is actually the case. Possibility, we would suggest, makes sense only in
the face of transcending formidible metaphysical limits and existential barriers, and next to nothing in a world where all things spiritual have been relativized and trivialized. Experientially devoid of
anything that might be termed a firm juxtaposition, we find ourselves cauterized by the one-dimensional world of our own making.

It is, therefore, not surprising that there should lately have been
advertised widely a "death of God." What of that which we once in
breathless awe named "Transcendence-Itself" could survive the
quantification of language and the massification of society so charac-
teristic of our time? Even the arts seem to have succumbed, as
Harold Rosenberg observes adroitly, no longer challenging us with
a "re" but with a "de-definition," [4] assuming their place obediently
alongside the rest of the fleshless apparatus of technocracy and becoming scarcely distinguishable from it. If B. F. Skinner's "Walden
II" is an accurate prognosis of future necessities, then, perforce
there can be room for neither gods nor devils; the mythic notion of
"freedom" is swallowed up by *Homo sapiens* become the "modu-
lar man" of "behavior modification," with computer art providing
the new—and in this context entirely "natural"—aesthetic *sine qua
non*. As Theodore Roszak has put it, "as we are on the inside, so
also the outside." [5] For the "cold vacancy" of Stevens' lament we
have no one to blame ultimately but ourselves.

Of late, however, there has been apparent a subtle shifting of
religious sentiments suggesting, perhaps, that there may still be occasion for a retrieval of the mytho-symbolic language of the spirit
—the development of what Roszak terms a "rhapsodic intellect." [6]

The popularity of college courses dealing with source materials in departments of religion and the surprising encroachment of the language of the spiritual into the offerings of philosophy and— "Saints preserve us!"—the behavioral sciences is now a well-established fact. There are, no doubt, a substantial number of theologians and religionists momentarily set scurrying by so-called secular theology who are now saying, "I told you so!" knowing all along what might happen if the gods should be offered up on the high altar of scientific positivism gone "pop."

If we are at all in touch with the foundations of human experience, we should have long since realized that if God and the Devil are to be known—to say nothing of believed—they must be known "figurally" and "mythically," that is, "humanly" and "personally," as realities both present to and arising out of human experience. Recognizing that our "time of need," as Heidegger put it, is perhaps "reaching its midpoint," scholars in religious and theological studies are taking a closer and more circumspect look at Bultmann's project of "demythologizing," denying not its overall validity and sophistication as a "method" of interpretation, but recognizing that the word "myth" is much too closely wedded to human experience to be taken lightly. And, of course, I am not here suggesting that Bultmann regarded myth lightly. The point is simply that the nature and meaning of myth cannot be fathomed any more than the nature and meaning of "man" can be so fathomed. One must not forget that the word-symbols "God" and "Devil," the "sacred" and the "profane," "good" and "evil," have their originating expression in *human* experience. Thus all attempts to provide an encompassing, systematic explanation for the nature and meaning of myth have failed and must fail. As Wolfhart Pannenberg suggests, to limit a religious text, symbol or myth to a single frame of interpretation at the expense of all others—even when that method limits itself to discerning the meaning of the text as a basic expression of human existence—"evidences an anthropological constriction of the question." [7] Panenberg accurately perceives, as does Paul Ricoeur, that the mythopoetic language of religious experience is far too fragile and delicate to lend itself to any method of interpretation that would remove it from its immediate context—the context of mythic time and space. Sounding a good deal more like Karl Jaspers who, in his explosive diatribe against Bultmann,[8] called for *re*-mythologizing rather than *de*-mythologizing religious language, Paul Ricoeur clarifies the matter by saying:

We must never speak of demythization but strictly of demythologizing, it being well understood that what is lost [suspended] is
the pseudo-knowledge, the false logos of myth, such as we find expressed, for example, in the etiological function of myth. But when
we lost the myth as immediate logos, we rediscover it as myth.[9]

In a word, simply because talk about gods and devils happens to
be "figural" and "mythic" in no way detracts from its truth and insight. Such language is killed—as is the spirit—only and always
when it is placed into straitjacketed explanations, the "logos" or
objectifying interpretation of which Ricoeur speaks. Far from being anti-personal, the hermeneutical stance suggested by Pannenberg and Ricoeur is profoundly personal, for it recognizes that only
when religious experience is authentically personal can its expressions force us to take it seriously. One cannot by fiat translate and
therefore encapsulate mere ideas and speculative abstractions into
the figural imagery of an enduring myth. Indeed, to what end? Simply to confound the reader? As Tillich has reminded us, the process
of religious symbolization is far more complex than the arbitrari-
ness of an isolated, albeit imaginative, individual wishing to develop the means of his own immortality.[10] The great symbols of
religion are forged out of the crucible of great experience—that is,
great *personal* experience. Sensing the same, Arthur Vogel writes
in his recent book:

> My position is the exact opposite of that described by the well-
> known psychologist Abraham Maslow, who has written that it is "in-
> creasingly developing that leading theologians and sophisticated peo-
> ple in general [!] define their God, not as a person, but as a force, a
> principle . . . of the whole of Being." . . . to deny the primacy of a
> personal God in favor of an impersonal principle or power seems
> [to me] the ultimate naiveté.[11]

At the risk of severe oversimplification, we might suggest that
the appeal of the "experientially" centered and highly "mythical"
religious movements that seem to be everywhere present these days
is, at least in part, a direct reaction against the intellectualization of
religion, whether in terms of meaning or principles. So powerful
has become the contemporary idol of abstractionism, so foreboding
the working lexicons of philosophers and theologians, and so burnt-
out the clergy who, as Roszak cogently observes, have been "scram-
bling for relevance" throughout the 1960's, that people (and

particularly young people) have defected from the traditional channels of religious communication. "Willful belief of the unbelievable," supported as it may be by a humanist, secular ethic, "was never better than a poor substitute for sacramental experience." [12]

But even though there are "signs of an odd return of the gods" and the rather more bizarre forms of religion in general one must, as Donald Carne-Ross puts it, "beware of religious stunting" as proof of its authenticity.[13] The banal and sensationalized publicity that has attended the film version of William Blatty's *The Exorcist* (about which E. V. Walter and John R. May speak at length in this collection), the revival of interest in the occult, witchcraft, astrology, and other forms of religious diversion (including many aspects of the charismatic, Neo-Pentecostalist movement), are all symptomatic of various kinds of contemporary religious faking.

At the same time, however, we contend that these various sociological and cultural phenomena are not at all unimportant or insignificant. Under the seeming naiveté of contemporary religious affectations, whether demonology, psychedelic mysticism or whatever, one can, we believe, extract religious underpinnings that are quite real; not least the fact that more and more very bright and perceptive people are coming around to the conviction of Arthur Vogel that "the personal God is the only God worth having." This growing shift in contemporary religious sentiment may have close to its heart the discovery of Teilhard de Chardin who, out of a searching conversation with the Whirlwind, says eloquently:

> You hoped that the more thoroughly you rejected the tangible, the closer you would be to spirit: that you would be more divine if you lived in the pure world of thought, or at least more angelic if you fled the corporeal? Well, you were like to have perished from hunger.[14]

If, in fact, it is a longing for experiential immediacy that underlies the new religious quest, then it is high time we tune ourselves to the language of, and not merely about, religion—the language of myth.

The essays in this collection were written, in part, as response to a contemporary religious phenomenon—in this case the double-sided issue of the Devil and the demonic—as an attempt to untangle and clarify some of the prevailing confusion concerning Satanism and demonology. But let the reader not be misled. Even though this collection is largely interpretive, in no way do its essayists intend a demythification of the demonic, if by that term is implied a mere explanation of the power of evil. Far from it. The writers of these essays have the utmost respect for the multifarious disguises of the demonic, whether cloaked in the figural imagery of myth and folk-lore, the depths of human consciousness, or the terrifying testimony of recent historical events. The guiding principle of selection has been to provide the reader with a variety of perspectives, whether historical, philosophical, theological, psychological, cultural or lit-erary, and *not* to provide uniform agreement on an issue so com-plex as the one before us. The essayists speak for themselves.

No attempt has been made to provide an over-arching schema for the organization of these essays into the harmony of a central thesis. Although there are distinct differences between evil con-strued as something encroaching upon us from without and beyond the human agency, and evil understood as something generated en-tirely within by way of an unholy or perverse will, one cannot, as both Professors Kohák and McGill suggest, make this into a final philosophical and hermeneutical demarcation. To opt, as it were, for either the external or internal point of view is to destroy by not taking seriously the integrity of the figurative, mythic language of the demonic. The essays have been placed, therefore, into a pattern which seems to provide a smooth and complementary narrative se-quence; not an argumentative progression.

It is interesting to note, finally, that as literature about the Devil reappears in our time, even the most scientific and presumably "ob-jective" minds turn to the mythic symbols of antiquity in order to make sense out of the reality of the demonic. But that should not surprise us, for religion wears a "human" face seeking expression through the language closest to it—the figural language of the body, the *poiesis* of the mythical. Beginning to recognize the inescapabil-ity of myth in one form or another, it may be that we are evidenc-ing a new and, hopefully, fruitful dialogue between contemporary and past forms of myth. Out of the impoverishment of material affluence and boredom, the oppressive transience of "instantaneous-ness" in practically all forms of mass culture and value, it may be that we are beginning to discover the insanity of "driving the ghost out of the machine" resonating once again to the echoes of other voices—the very phantoms of Stevens' thought long dead. If the new encounter proves to be superficial and abortive, then we will be so much the poorer, for, as Gerhard Ebeling has reminded us, the elimination of the mythopoetic creates a *sepsis*—a "poisoning" of human language. Talk of, about, and indeed to the gods "is necessary to life itself . . . as the only language that can preserve its humanity." [15]

Collectively, the essays warn us of the danger of looking for the Devil only in the dark caverns of human experience. It is not that the Devil, and even the demonic, cannot be dislodged from the esoteric and cryptic abodes of nature and history, cosmos and psyche, but if we are really serious about the matter we must look more closely to ourselves for, as William Woods puts it,

> The primordial things are commonplace, frog voices in the pond, crickets, a bull bellowing, the sun climbing up out of the bracken high over Red Hill. If we understand this we have begun to see our ideas of causality in perspective and become part not only of the past, but of both God and devil, for it is in these things that God and the devil were born and where they live.[16]

The Devil's name is "Legion," his disguises are manifold and we are several.

NOTES

1. Wallace Stevens, "Esthétique de Mal," VIII, *The Collected Poems of Wallace Stevens*, (New York: Alfred A. Knopf, Inc.). Copyright 1947 by Wallace Stevens. Used by permission.

2. *Ibid.*

3. On this, see Nathan Scott, Jr., *The Wild Prayer of Longing: Poetry and the Sacred* (New Haven: Yale University Press, 1971), pp. 1–42.

4. Harold Rosenberg, *The De-definition of Art* (New York: Collier, 1972).

5. Theodore Roszak, *Where the Wasteland Ends: Politics and Transcendence in Postindustrial Society* (New York: Doubleday, 1973).

6. *Ibid.*

7. Wolfhart Pannenberg, *Basic Questions in Theology*, I, trans. George H. Kehm (Philadelphia: Fortress Press, 1970), pp. 110–111.

8. Karl Jaspers and Rudolf Bultmann, *Myth and Christianity*, trans. Norbert Guterman (New York: Noonday Press, 1958).

9. Paul Ricoeur, *The Symbolism of Evil*, trans. Emerson Buchanan (New York: Harper and Row, 1967), p. 162.

10. Paul Tillich, *Theology of Culture* (New York: Oxford, 1959), pp. 53–67; and *Dynamics of Faith* (New York: Harper and Row, 1957), pp. 41–54.

11. Arthur Vogel, *Body Theology: God's Presence in Man's World* (New York: Harper and Row, 1973), p. 5.

12. Roszak, *op. cit.*, pp. 449–451.

13. *Cf.* essay by Donald Carne-Ross entitled "Classics and the Intellectual Community," *Arion*, New Series 1/1, Spring, 1973, pp. 7–66.

14. Teilhard de Chardin, *Hymn of the Universe*, trans. Gerald Vann (New York: Harper and Row, 1969), pp. 63–64.

15. Gerhard Ebeling, *God and Word*, trans. James Leitch (Philadelphia: Fortress Press, 1967), p. 49. See also the recent work of Ebeling entitled, *Introduction to a Theological Theory of Language*, trans. R. A. Wilson (Philadelphia: Fortress Press, 1973), for an extended discussion of the same.

16. William Woods, *A History of the Devil* (New York: Putnam, 1973), p. 233.

E. V. Walter

DEMONS AND DISENCHANTMENT

BORN EAST OF THE MEDITERRANEAN SEA, Satan grew up in Europe. Occidental images and ideas shaped his form and substance. The present wave of interest in the demonic, however, tends to recede from Western iconography and theology and flow toward the symbolism of primitive and archaic societies as well as the sacromagical traditions of other civilizations. William Peter Blatty, in his enormously popular novel, *The Exorcist*, exhibits not the Devil of the Western imagination but a great demon he names "Pazuzu," who, according to his story, had been worshipped as a god in ancient Mesopotamia. In the film based on the novel, clever cinematography briefly but effectively exploits the mystery and power of Babylonian imagery.

This essay explores the relationship between the present interest in the demonic and the quest for re-enchantment. It also examines the meaning of demonic experience and the practice of exorcism in the time before the disenchantment of the world.

I

Since the time when Max Weber identified "intellectualization," "rationalization," and "the disenchantment of the world" as an overwhelming trend of Western civilization, countermovements resisting that trend have gathered strength and shown unexpected endurance. To some extent, the revival of demonology and what is called "the occult," as well as the interest in exotic religions, may be understood as part of the resistance. But there is also another way of looking at it. The Occident is deprived of rationales for demonic experience. All Western religions—including the Roman

17

Catholic Church, despite its tradition of guarding the idiom of supernatural experience—have been caught up in the great movement of disenchantment. Now they all take positions of skepticism in relation to phenomena that *appear* to be caused by supernatural, magical, or demonic forces. Their primary rationales for these appearances are not different from the scientific rationales of secular people. Reluctantly, when the secular, disenchanted concepts are exhausted or proved inadequate, they will shift to the complementary idiom. Therefore, sacromagical words and practices have become secondary rationales—expressions of last resort. Officially, then, even the churches make it difficult to *believe* in demons. By withholding the symbols of demonology from the experience of the demonic, they diminish the reality of demons. Against this progressive demystification of the traditional Western religions, we are presently witnessing the revolt of the disenchanted.

Since it is no longer reasonable or respectable to believe in demons, the sense of the demonic and the feelings associated with demonic encounters seek expression in ideas and images outside Occidental traditions. The present interest in exotic religions and occult idioms, then, may be understood as much more than the latest trick played by quirky fashion or by the cunning of unreason. Instead, it is inspired by a serious search for appropriate modes of expression in an extensive quest for re-enchantment. At the moment, a significant figure in that movement is a Yaqui Indian sorcerer, Castaneda's don Juan.* Yet many readers rush to believe that he is entirely a literary invention, so eager are they to turn don Juan into a "mere myth" of the quest for re-enchantment.

The present mood might be named neo-heterodoxy, as the mood

---

* Carlos Castaneda, a young professor of anthropology at UCLA, recently has become the subject of considerable interest and acclaim in both the academic and popular press (*cf.* feature stories in *Time*, Mar. 5, 1973 and *Harpers*, Feb. 1973, Sept. 1974. A great deal of his appeal seems due to the fact that Castaneda's writings are highly "personal" and presumably autobiographical. Living as obscurely and mysteriously as he writes, Castaneda clearly participates in his religious quest and does not merely theorize about it. While his first two books, *viz.*, *The Teachings of Don Juan* (1968) and *A Separate Reality* (1971), represent published versions of Castaneda's now famous "field notes," his later work, *Journey to Ixtlan* (1972), brilliantly illustrates the author's ability to represent the classic patterns of mysticism and the occult through a genre of literature that speaks compellingly to the contemporary situation. Among those actively endeavoring to "re-enchant" the disenchanted West, Castaneda is rapidly becoming one of the more influential voices. (Ed.)

of the previous generation was named neo-orthodoxy. Both moods have in common a revolt from the optimism and progressivism of a previous era, and a serious effort to recover and to express experiences that had been submerged in the wake of disenchantment. Neo-orthodoxy explored the dimensions of original sin, but retained a Christian theological framework. Neo-heterodoxy revives the ancient victims of historic Christianity, fetching from oblivion sorcery, magic, witchcraft, along with forgotten heresies and forbidden gods. Old pagan and heathen representations not only float out of the earth but threaten to bury their undertakers.

It is difficult for us to recreate, even in imagination, the intellectual mood of a man like Henry Thomas Buckle—a renowned historian and the model of Victorian evolutionary optimism—who assured us in the 11th edition of the *Encyclopaedia Britannica* that we would soon be enjoying life in a civilization ". . . freed from the last ghost of superstition—an Age of Reason in which mankind shall at last find refuge from the hosts of occult and invisible powers, the fearsome galaxies of deities and demons, which have haunted him thus far at every stage of his long journey through savagery, barbarism and civilization."

II

The campaign against superstition has always made its first offensive against the sense of the demonic and the fear of demons. The Greeks had a word for a certain dimension of sacromagical, numinous experience, *deisidaimonia*, which may be translated as "demon dread." Greek rationalistic thinkers of the fourth century B.C. and afterward identified this term with "superstition." Plutarch in his essay, *Peri deisidaimonias*, condemned it because he wanted religion to offer comfort and not fright. In the mind of the superstitious man, he wrote, reason is always dreaming while fear is always awake. Jane Harrison observed that Plutarch, like others more rationalistic than he, rejected the dark side of religious experience entirely: "Unable to see the good side of the religion of fear, unable to realize that in it was implicit a real truth, the consciousness that all is not well with the world, that there is such a thing as evil." [1] In the sixth century before the Christian era, Harrison pointed out, *deisidaimonia* had been not mere superstition, but a genuine sacromagical experience that worshipped

not rational, human, law-abiding *gods*, but vague, irrational, mainly
malevolent (*daimones*), spirit-things, ghosts and bogeys and the like,
not yet formulated and enclosed into god-head. The word (*deisidaimonia*) tells its own tale, but the thing itself was born long before
it was baptized.

That thing itself, "demon dread," constituted the central element
in the religious experience of the most ancient civilization we know
from historical records: the Sumerian-Babylonian-Assyrian people.[2]
It also appeared in ancient Egypt, which was cheerful, optimistic,
and much less demon-ridden than the Mesopotamian civilization. A
Greek alchemical papyrus describing the practice of bonesetting in
Egyptian medicine, mentions two kinds of bonesetter. One operated
"mechanically" (*mechanikos*) and set fractures "by the book" (*apo
bibliou*). The other was an exorcist and worked through supernatural inspiration and his own personal *deisidaimonia*—his own demonic sensitivity. According to the papyrus, the exorcist type of
bonesetter was so effective that one could hear the creaking of the
bones as they mended.[3]

In ancient Greece, the experience of the demonic, which found
expression in the religious idiom of the sixth and fifth centuries
B.C., was obscured in the disenchantment of the succeeding centuries, only to recover its importance in the Hellenistic world—
especially in the first century A.D. in Rome and elsewhere.[4] Within
paganism, the philosophers re-enchanted their universe, opening
philosophical discourse to all kinds of mystical and occult systems.
Within Christianity, the demonic element remained at the center of
religious experience until modern times—or at least until the
Enlightenment.

The recent film *The Exorcist* exploits the *deisidaimonia* of a disenchanted public. It also exploits the climax of the novel, sacrificing everything to the scene in which two priests, reading from the
Roman Ritual, engage in a gigantic struggle to free a child from
possession by a great demon. The lurid sensationalism of the film
has eclipsed a number of serious issues in the novel. The book represents the ambiguity of Roman Catholic culture in the throes of
disenchantment after Vatican II. The hero, Father Karras, who is a
Jesuit as well as a psychiatrist, is committed to the rationales of
both the Church and secular psychodynamics. He suffers a crisis of
faith, which is not really generated by a conflict between religion
and science, but recalls the spiritual travail of Ivan Karamazov and

of Camus' hero in *The Fall*. Since integrity of faith is required in an exorcist, the dramatic function of his crisis is to render him unfit to perform the Ritual himself. The venerable Merrin, who had actually struggled with this demon years before in Africa, is summoned to perform, with Karras assisting. Merrin's heart attack leaves the exorcism incomplete, and moves Karras to challenge the demon to enter himself, thereby releasing the child. Ironically, Karras gains salvation in a suicidal plunge, winning the life of the child by sacrificing his own.

The exorcism scene is a violent, room-shaking, furniture-thumping, body-racking conflict between priests and demon, but another kind of tension has built up to it—the tension between the rationales of scientific psychiatry on the one hand, and the sacromagical tradition in Catholicism on the other hand. Progressively learning that the child is possessed, the reader—like the mother in the book—grows impatient with the hesitation of the clergy, and demands that psychiatric interpretation be swept aside, and the case delivered to an exorcist without further delay. The claims of exorcism against the claims of psychiatry to define the situation generate this tension. Is possession a disguise for psychosis—or vice versa? Indeed, the high dramatic intensity of the book depends on the historic disenchantment of the Church and the official position of exorcism as a last resort.

III

In a previous age, when it was a first resort, exorcism was easier. Explosive, world-shaking struggles with demons were known, but were not common, presumably because exorcists had more power in the old days. Sometimes, it was said, demons would turn tail and flee at the mere approach of an exorcist. In the first half of the fourth century, Julius Firmicus Maternus, a writer during the reigns of Constantine the Great and his sons, described exorcists as:

> Men terrible to the gods [and] terrible to all demons, and at their approach the wicked spirits of demons flee; and they free men who are thus troubled, not by force of words but by their mere appearing; and however violent the demon may be who shakes the body and spirit of man, whether he be aerial or terrestrial or infernal, he flees at the bidding of this sort of man and fears his precepts with a certain veneration. These are they who are called exorcists by the people.[5]

Still earlier, at the beginning of the third century, Tertullian had described the easy power of Christians over demons. He claimed that only Christians could really expel demons from men's bodies, and that they were sought eagerly by high and low to drive the demons out. He demanded of the pagan critics who wanted to suppress the Christian community:

> Who would deliver you from those secret foes, ever busy both destroying your souls and ruining your health? Who would save you, I mean, from the attacks of those spirits of evil, which without reward or hire we exorcise? [6]

Christ gave his followers authority over demons, and the servants of Christ reminded the evil spirits of their impending punishment:

> So at our touch and breathing, overwhelmed by the thought and realization of those judgment fires, they leave at our command the bodies they have entered, unwilling, and distressed, and before your very eyes put to an open shame.[6]

In the century before, Justin Martyr had written that Christian exorcism worked effectively among all people, even where other methods failed.

In the early centuries, any Christian had the authority and the capacity to exorcise demons from the possessed. The most adept placed themselves in the service of the afflicted, challenging demonic forces with the confidence of superior athletes.

St. Paul had established the idiom and imagery of the conflict in Ephesians 6:12. Christians must grapple with the forces of evil. They wrestled with demons. As the Douay Bible put it: "For our wrestling is not against flesh and blood: but against principalities and powers, against the rulers of the world of this darkness, against the spirits of wickedness in the high places." In the Vulgate, Jerome chose *conluctatio*, which means "wrestling," to translate Paul's original Greek. The word Paul had chosen was *palé*, which also means "wrestling"—a precise choice because it is the only time that word is used in the New Testament. Paul defined the Christian struggle with demonic energy not as an impersonal conflict against abstract forces or even as a battle with a faceless enemy, but as a personal, intimate, sweaty, hand-to-hand combat.

Throughout the Middle Ages, the intimate enemy—represented by demons and diabolic agents—was everywhere. Historian Henry Charles Lea observed, "We cannot understand the motives and acts of our forefathers unless we take into consideration the mental condition engendered by the consciousnees of . . . daily and hourly personal conflict with Satan." [7] Yet, as men lived in the constant presence of demons, the sense of danger was often relieved by confidence in the power of sacred words and holy names to control them. Demons were wicked, harmful entities, but not always terrifying, and sometimes worthy only of contempt. One story of a whimpering demon was passed on for centuries. It seems that a nun went into the garden and—neglecting to make the sign of the cross before she ate a piece of lettuce—swallowed a demon perched on the lettuce leaf. In due course, an exorist was called to treat her as a victim of accidental possession. When the exorcist drew the evil spirit forth and heaped maledictions on him, the demon complained that he was not to blame—he had been sitting on that lettuce in the garden doing harm to no one, when, before he could get out of the way, she came along and ate him!

Lecky, the historian of European morals, reminds us that the most striking change in the past three centuries may be found in the common response to the idea of the miraculous or the supernatural. Now, when the spirit of rationalism predisposes men to attribute all kinds of phenomena to natural rather than to miraculous causes, the account of a miracle or any other supernatural event draws "an absolute and even derisive incredulity which dispenses with all examination of the evidence." To ascribe unexplainable phenomena to supernatural agency "is beyond the range of reasonable discussion." In contrast, a few centuries ago, miraculous and preternatural accounts were not only credible but quite ordinary. [8]

IV

Under the impact of this change, the Roman Catholic Church has modified the occasions for exorcism and the conditions, even though the procedures of exorcism and the theory of demonic possession remain unchanged in principle. The passage from first to last resort has changed the *context* of exorcism. Demons, having receded from constant, intimate presence, are experienced as occasional, alien entities. The clergy are more comfortable with psychological abnormalities than with diabolic possession. They no longer grapple with demons.

This disenchantment may be illustrated by comparing *The Catholic Encyclopedia* of 1907 with *The New Catholic Encyclopedia*, published exactly sixty years later.[9] In 1907, the Church, still struggling with the heresy of Modernism, opposed the emancipation of the sciences and the adaptation of the Church to modern thought. In the words of the new Encyclopedia, "Only after World War II did a trend emerge toward a renewed consideration of subjects that had been so destructively and abortively handled by the Modernists." [10] Only then did the Church feel comfortable with secular psychodynamics and with the autonomy of science.

By directly comparing their articles on "demons," "demoniacs," "diabolic possession," and "exorcism," one may discern little more than a subtle difference in the two encyclopedias.[11] The old Encyclopedia pointed out that the bishop's authority was usually required before exorcism might be attempted, and cautioned: "Possession is not lightly to be taken for granted. Each case is to be carefully examined and great caution to be used in distinguishing genuine possession from certain forms of disease." (Vol. V, p. 712.) Still, the old Encyclopedia warned against rationalistic rejections of the possibility of possession, and observed: "A careful consideration of the medical aspect of demonic possession has often been associated with a denial of the demonic agency. But this is by no means necessary; and, rightly understood, the medical evidence may even help to establish the truth of the record." (Vol. IV, p. 713.)

The new Encyclopedia, by contrast, gives more emphasis to psychiatric interpretation:

> Psychiatry . . . has shown that the workings of the subconscious explain many, if not most, of the abnormal conditions that earlier generations had attributed to diabolical activity. For these reasons and because the need to reorient theology along more positive lines has been recognized, demonology has not been the object of very much serious study in the 20th century. (Vol. IV, p. 756.)

The rite of exorcism has lost its ancient status as the first offensive weapon against demonic forces. By so stringently regulating the manner of dealing with the possibility of diabolic possession, the Church reduced the opportunities for those intimate, personal, wrestling matches with evil forces long familiar to traditional Christian experience. This change in the conditions, however, is part of a much larger transformation of the context of exorcism.

The new Encyclopedia omits entirely two articles which appeared in the old Encyclopedia—an article on "adjuration" and a briefer one on "malediction." This change is not subtle at all, and it marks the disenchantment of Roman Catholic consciousness—along with the disenchantment of other Occidental religions. Exorcism remains, but to all intents and purposes *sui generis*, whereas in the ancient and medieval context it was known as only one species in a large genus of adjurations. Unless we understand the grand pattern of sacromagical ritual, which once included exorcism in a complex design of adjurations, blessings, and formal curses, we shall not grasp the modes in which men grappled with evil before the disenchantment of the world.

The story of *The Exorcist* hinges on the power of Title XII in the *Roman Ritual* to liberate the child from possession. Actually, Title XII is a formal procedure of solemn adjuration, to be performed by a qualified exorcist, but it is not the only method for dealing with cases of possession. Exorcism by private adjuration is still open to any Christian. Solemn adjuration is the ritual exorcism now performed by ordained ministers with specific episcopal permission. An adjuration is a request or a command for some kind of action in the name of a divine person. The New Testament contains a number of passages that support the Christian rationale for adjuration. In John 14:13, Christ says, "Whatsoever you shall ask the Father in My name, that will I do: that the Father may be glorified in the Son." In Mark 16:17, Jesus says, "In My name they shall cast out devils." Adjurations were either imprecatory or deprecatory, generally speaking, but demons were adjured exclusively in the language of enmity and command. Exorcism was simply a form of expulsion by adjuration in the name of God or Christ. The sacred names carried a power that demons could not resist.

The power of sacred names was especially important in the ritual curses known as anathemas and maledictions. The article on "anathema," extending to three columns in the old Encyclopedia, is reduced to a mere fifteen lines in the new Encyclopedia—another significant modification. Moreover, this curtailed statement describes "anathema" as a synonym for "excommunication," thus distorting its older meaning. The social and ecclesiastical effects of excommunication must be distinguished from the power of anathema as a ritual curse. The original meaning of anathema referred to things declared execrable and set apart for divine destruction. Later, in Christendom, it signified exclusion from the community, but frequently included covering the object with sacred curses or maledictions. The procedure of excommunication did indeed include formulas of anathema and malediction, but those formulas, far from being synonymous with excommunication, were independent and separable. Exorcists recited anathemas and maledictions against the Devil and his demons, but they did not excommunicate them, because excommunication could be inflicted only on baptized, living persons who were members of the Church. Even animals, we shall see, were targets of anathema and malediction. Excommunication, therefore, contained two elements: formal exclusion from the communion of the faithful on the one hand, and the ritual curse on the other hand. When a medieval exorcist announced to an insect or an animal, "I excommunicate you!" he was referring exclusively to the ritual curse and invoking the power of sacred adjuration.

The new perspective that inspires the *New Catholic Encyclopedia* drops "adjurations," "anathemas" and "maledictions" as unimportant fossils, but before disenchantment they were powerful forces worked into the fabric of everyday life. Here is an example of one seventh-century anathema against thieves to illustrate the rhetorical power of the formula, to say nothing of its sacromagical efficacy:

> Cursed be they in the town and cursed in the field, Amen! Cursed be they in their houses and cursed in their farms, Amen! Cursed be they in the forests and cursed in the waters, Amen! Cursed be they in the roads and cursed in the streets, and in all places, Amen! Unless they amend let them be involved in manifold maledictions, Amen! Let no priest visit them when dying, nor be they buried in holy ground, but be cast out as stinking corpses, Amen! Cursed be their granaries and cursed be what they leave, Amen! Cursed be they in going out and cursed in coming in, Amen! May the Lord strike them with want, with fever, with cold, with heat, with thirst, and persecute them until they perish, Amen! And as this candle is extinguished in the eyes of men, so may their light be extinguished in eternity, Amen! [12]

The formula of malediction was just as powerful as the anathema. Here is an example of a malediction, rich in imagination and detail.

Let him be accursed wherever he be, whether at home or abroad, in the road or in the path, or in the wood, or in the water, or in the church. Let him be accursed living and dying, eating, drinking, fasting or athirst, slumbering, sleeping, waking, walking, standing, sitting, lying, working, idling . . . and bleeding. Let him be accursed in all the forces of his body. Let him be accursed outside and inside; accursed in his hair and accursed in his brain; accursed in the crown of his head, in his temples, in his forehead, in his ears, in his brows, in his eyes, in his cheeks, in his jaws, in his nostrils, in his front teeth, in his back teeth, in his lips, in his throat, in his shoulders, in his upper arms, in his lower arms, in his hands, in his fingers, in his breast, in his heart, in his stomach and liver, in his kidneys, in his loins, in his hips, in his [genitals], in his thighs, in his knees, in his shins, in his feet, in his toes, and in his nails. Let him be accursed in every joint of his body. Let there be no health in him, from the crown of his head to the sole of his foot. May Christ, the Son of the Living God, curse him throughout His Kingdom, and may Heaven with all its Virtues rise up against him to his damnation, unless he repents and renders due satisfaction. Amen. So be it. So be it. Amen.[13]

Anathemas and maledictions in the form of excommunications became matters of routine, and administrators resorted to them on almost any occasion. In the early part of the twelfth century, the Archbishop of Compostela must have given enormous confidence to his librarian when he fulminated an excommunication that consigned to eternal damnation any culprit who might steal or mutilate the precious manuscripts in his cathedral archives. And what modern-day university administrator, concerned about the soaring costs of student housing, would not envy the spiritual rent control enjoyed by Pope Clement III, in the twelfth century. To assist the recently established University of Bologna, he issued a bull declaring anathema any landlord who might raise the rent of teachers or students.[14]

All kinds of ritual procedures were used interchangeably as defenses and facilitations in the business of living. The principle of excommunication (denying the sacraments to unworthy members of the religious community) tended to become obscured by the secondary notion of a ban, curse, or interdict directed not only against persons, but also against animals, plants, such as weeds in a garden, or even inanimate objects. The historical record reveals hundreds of cases in which plagues and scourges of vermin were dispersed by excommunicatory procedures. In most cases, they

41719

withdrew from the fields to the special places or reservations prescribed by the bishop. In 1451, the leeches threatened to destroy the fish in Lake Geneva. After a regular trial in the episcopal court, the leeches retired, under pain of excommunication by the Bishop of Lausanne, to a certain area of the Lake, where they remained within limits. In the thirteenth century, the mosquitoes of Mayence, because of their tiny bodies and extreme youth, had a curator appointed for them, who persuaded the court to give them a piece of land to which they were banished. In the sixteenth century, a Spanish bishop ordered all the rats and mice to swim in vast numbers to an island assigned to them. As late as 1713 in Brazil an immense colony of ants, after a regular trial and after the sentence was read at the entrance of every visible ant hole, marched to a special place reserved for them under pain of excommunication. The sentence in an earlier French case known as the *People versus Locusts*, ordered "the aforesaid locusts and grasshoppers and other animals by whatsoever name they may be called, under pain of malediction and anathema to depart from the vineyards and fields of this district within six days from the publication of this sentence and to do no further damage there or elsewhere." [15] It resembled the form of excommunication described by Bartholomew Chasseneux: "O snails, caterpillars, and other obscene creatures, which destroy the food of our neighbours, depart hence! Leave these cantons which you are devastating, and take refuge in those localities where you can injure no one." [16] According to Evans, no one appeared "to have doubted for a moment that the Church could, by virtue of its anathema, compel these creatures to stop their ravages and cause them to go from one place to another. Indeed, a firm faith in the existence of this power was the pivot on which the whole procedure turned, and without it, the trial would have been a dismal farce in the eyes of all who took part in it." [17]

So common were such ecclesiastical actions, indeed, that elaborate trial procedures were drawn up to make certain that the rights of invading insects and animals were scrupulously observed. Karl von Amira, a historian of law, writing at the end of the 19th century, showed that these ecclesiastical animal trials remain unintelligible unless we think in terms of medieval demonology.[18] The trials depended on the formal adjurations of *maledictio*, anathema, and exorcism. The formulas were directed not primarily at the animals on trial, but at the evil spirits believed to inhabit them.

By the end of the seventeenth century, animal trials were considered absurd, and they disappeared about the same time that trials for witchcraft came to an end. Mechanistic principles and naturalistic ideas replaced the animistic perspective, which had supported a world filled with demons. Nevertheless, as Gaston Bachelard has observed, the intellectual transformation that produced the disenchantment of the world and inspired the scientific world view may also be understood as a spiritual revolution.[19]

V

A sense of the demonic presence endures, despite all rationalistic efforts to deny it. Disenchanted ideas, having made their descent to the inactive commonplace—to use Whitehead's terms—obscure more than they reveal about the meaning of evil in our excruciating world. However, we are living through a change in the habits of rational thought. Previously, it was a habit to deny the notion of the demonic by demonstrating its absurdity *a priori* in the terms of disenchanted vocabularies. The new attitude would seek not to deny the demonic, but to ask what it means. It would enlarge our understanding of the scope of the demonic and the range of circumstances to which it is relevant.

Until recently, reasonable people believed that the fundamental ideas which illumine human experience extinguish one another in historical progression. Here, we have tried to rescue some old ideas from obscurity, recognizing that antique notions are not necessarily extinct. Revived in a new context, they may enlarge our understanding of the demonic as an incorrigible experience.

Today, people are reaching beyond disenchantment in other ways as well. Perhaps we are on the brink of another spiritual revolution, which will inspire a new map of experience, rendering obsolete the old boundaries that separated the worlds of magic, religion, and science.

In the words of don Juan, reported by Castaneda, "Perhaps you know now that *seeing* happens only when one sneaks between the worlds, the world of ordinary people and the world of sorcerers." [20] Perhaps if we discard the conceit that we can see through each of those worlds, we may hope for the vision that enables us to see between them.

NOTES

1. Jane Harrison, *Prolegomena to the Study of Greek Religion* (New York: Meridian, 1957), pp. 6–7.

2. See Henri Frankfort, *The Birth of Civilization in the Near East* (New York: Doubleday Anchor book, 1959).

3. G. Maspero, Note on "L'art et Mystère du médecin qui connaît la marche du coeur . . ." *Proceedings of the Society of Biblical Archaeology*, Vol. XIII (1891), pp. 501–502.

4. See G. W. Bowersock, *Greek Sophists in the Roman Empire* (Oxford: Clarendon Press, 1969). Ramsay Macmullen, *Enemies of the Roman Order* (Cambridge, Mass.: Harvard University Press, 1967).

5. Lynn Thorndike, *A History of Magic and Experimental Science.* 8 vols. (New York: Columbia University Press, 1923–58), Vol. I, p. 534.

6. Tertullian, *Writings.* Trans. A. Roberts and J. Donaldson (Edinburgh: T. & T. Clark, 1869), Vol. I, pp. 39, 4, 117, 101.

7. H. C. Lea, *A History of the Inquisition of the Middle Ages.* 3 vols. (New York: Russell, 1956), Vol. III, p. 382. First pub. 1887.

8. W. E. H. Lecky, *History of the Rise and Influence of the Spirit of Rationalism in Europe.* 2 vols. (New York: Appleton, 1868), Vol. I, pp. 17, 27.

9. *The Catholic Encyclopedia* (New York: Gilmary Society, 1907). *New Catholic Encyclopedia* (New York: McGraw-Hill, 1967).

10. *New Catholic Encyclopedia*, Vol. IX, p. 995.

11. *The Catholic Encyclopedia*, Vols. IV, V; *New Catholic Encyclopedia*, Vols. IV, V.

12. H. C. Lea, *Studies in Church History* (Philadelphia: Lea's Son & Co., 1883), p. 303.

13. *Ibid.*, p. 346.

14. *Ibid.*, pp. 435–436.

15. E. P. Evans, *The Criminal Prosecution and Capital Punishment of Animals* (New York: Dutton, 1906), p. 107.

16. S. Baring-Gould, *Curiosities of Olden Times.* Rev. ed. (Edinburgh: Grant, 1896), p. 64.

17. Evans, *op. cit.*, p. 50.

18. Karl von Amira, *Thierstrafen und Thierprocesse.* (Innsbruck: Wagner, 1891). I offer an interpretation of animal prosecutions and their implications in my essay, "Nature on Trial: The Case of the Rooster that Laid an Egg," to be published in *Boston Studies in the Philosophy of Science.*

19. Gaston Bachelard, *La formation de l'esprit scientifique*, 6th ed. (Paris: J. Vrin, 1969).

20. Carlos Castaneda, *Journey to Ixtlan* (New York: Simon and Schuster, 1973), p. 300.

John R. May

AMERICAN LITERARY VARIATIONS
ON THE DEMONIC

UPON RELEASING the film version in 1973 of William Peter Blatty's *The Exorcist* to American distributors, Warner Brothers issued a 23-page booklet of background material on exorcism, including a brief history of the rite, mention of some recent cases of demonic possession, a statement on science vis-à-vis the phenomenon, as well as reproduced copies of assorted newspaper articles dating back to *The Washington Post* story of August 20, 1949 reporting the case of the reputedly "possessed" Mt. Ranier boy, on which Blatty based his novel. The studio considered this "pertinent historical material" advisable inasmuch as a recent poll conducted by *Reader's Digest* had revealed that "more than 80 per cent of the U.S. public did not know the meaning of the word 'exorcist,' including a majority of those who had read the book." [1] The assumption of the brochure seems to be that the public needs only slight technical instruction in order to appreciate the film's explicit treatment of material of otherwise general interest. What the need for background material actually implies is that the public needs to be instructed in a sufficiently rare, and perhaps dubious, phenomenon in order to be taken in by a bizarre commercial venture under the guise of a significant cultural trend.

The background material has this to say about novelist and director respectively:

> By charting the specific symptoms of a young girl presumed "possessed" and detailing the methods by which the demon was exorcised from her, Blatty hoped to frame the unending battle between good and evil in a dramatically compelling and philosophically provocative narrative. Director William Friedkin's film version of *The Exorcist* has the same goal: to look realistically at the inexplic-

able events during a thoroughly documented, bizarre outbreak of evil
in one contemporary American home.[2]

The critics however have almost unanimously decided to pinpoint
the origin of this "bizarre outbreak of evil" somewhere in the abuse
of the free enterprise system, more specifically in the interplay of
novelist, studio and director. Pauline Kael, considered by many to
be the dean of American film critics, did not hesitate to assert that
"religious people . . . should be most offended by this movie," [3]
while accusing the Catholic Church of scoring a cinematic victory
second only to *The Bells of St. Mary's*. Vincent Canby labeled
Friedkin's film "a chunk of elegant occultist claptrap" and suggested that the $10 million budget for the film "could have been
better spent subsidizing a couple of beds at the Paine-Whitney
Clinic." [4]

It is scarcely surprising that what in these "last late days" faith
has apparently been unable to sustain, crass commercialism has exploited with financial, if not fiducial, success. One with at least
some vestige of confessional sensibility will indeed wonder why the
inhabitants of the secular city are such reeds shaken by the wind
that they cannot discern the sinister crackling of concealed Federal
Reserve notes for what earlier generations would have rightly taken
to be a suggestion of infernal fires.

When author, producer and director, with varying pastoral disguises for their shared profit motive, offer us cinema's most lu-
bricious pastiche of four-letter words and gross visual obscenities
while self-righteously asking their audience to wear the shoe if it
fits, one is inclined to think not so much of the dawn of a new age
of religious imagery as of the very "last lights off the black West." [5]

The resurgence of mass interest in the demonic has even affected
the field of hard-core pornography. Gerard Damiano's *Devil in
Miss Jones* (1973) has been advertised and even praised critically
as the best-made and most intelligent piece of cinematic pornography to have appeared to date. The quality of the film as cinema
has not of course compensated sufficiently for its obvious prurience
to have conferred upon it any redeeming social value. Miss Jones's
only mistake in life had been to terminate her own; and so Mr.
Abaca (who should have been called "Abraca," since his function
is pure Abracadabra), a sort of receptionist for the devil, permits
her to turn to life long enough to develop an adequate reason for
going below—namely, lust—because the punishment for suicide

hardly seems to fit the crime. What follows for the remaining hour, short of the brief final sequence, actually abuses the devil. The film's only redeeming intellectual allusion imagines the devil as a Sartrian fly who is known clearly to the inmates only in the specks that he leaves behind, but who may be expected to return if they pretend their eyes are closed. Hell for Miss Jones is being unable to achieve orgasm unaided; the film's obscene final pun has her male companion exclusively concerned with whether the devil will come.

That interest in the occult as a subcultural phenomenon has grown alarmingly in the last decade and continues to proliferate can be confirmed by even the most cursory perusal of metropolitan bookstores, but the so-called scientific approach is fortunately still limited in appeal. Paperback book sales and cinema more than television have accounted recently though for the general popularity of certain self-styled works of the imagination, e.g., Ira Levin's *Rosemary's Baby* (1967), Thomas Tryon's *The Other* (1971), and *The Exorcist* (1971).[6] The question that perplexes the analyst of literary trends in the face of this recent exposure to the supernatural is the one that George and Martha confront in Edward Albee's *Who's Afraid of Virginia Woolf?* "Truth or Illusion?" My assumption here will be that the problem of assessing the value of these works as literature can be distinguished from the issue concerning their place in American literary trends, and it is with the latter problem that I am principally concerned, since the former case is, for me at least, easily dismissed.

I

Are we faced with a genuine recurrence of the figural imagination in an age that has generally accepted its decline, if not demise? Nathan Scott has called ours "a world, indeed, which, being independent of any *other* worldly plan or scheme of meaning, has ceased to be a *figura* of anything extrinsic to itself and is sealed off against any transcendental ingress from without."[7] How, indeed, do we comprehend the terms *"figura"* and "figural," and their dialectical counterpart *persona*, which are the very bases of this analysis of the reemergence of the demon in contemporary literature? The term "figural," derived from the Latin *figura*, establishes a connection between a person or event within history that prefigures or "mirrors" another person or event, within or outside history (Scott implies a global figuralism in the latter sense), but in such a way that the first signifies both itself and the second while the second fulfills the first.[8] For example, in the Christian tradition Isaac is a *figura* of Christ; the last supper of Jesus, a *figura* of the Eternal Banquet. A figural view of reality suggests both a providentially directed history as well as the fulfillment of history outside time. Although figuralism in the Christian context is usually grounded on a traditional eschatological model, I feel that it may be extended to include less specifically the prefiguration of the ultimate revelation (however it may be made) of whatever endures as "mystery" in human existence.

The term *persona* by contrast, refers to any literary characterization, being used originally to designate the *personae* of a drama. To qualify as *persona*, however, it is not necessary for the character to be visually present to the fictional or real audience, for the term may be used of any effort to portray the existence of an independent personality through remembered or immediate sense experience. The gods were *dramatis personae* in the Greek theatre; the Bible consistently represents the experience of God speaking. Today, by extreme contrast, the supernatural or preternatural is conspicuously absent from literature—apart from the phenomenon under discussion here.

In short, what is important in this discrimination between *figura* and *persona* is that the former refers to a highly "intrinsic" representation of ultimate reality that always at least suggests the "mysterious" or awesome (in this case, the experience of the demonic within man or within human society), whether or not one believes that this reality has precise transhistorical or metaphysical referents. The latter term, by contrast, is largely an "extrinsic" rendering of the same reality whereby some of the deepest and most profound dimensions of the human experience are dissolved into abstractions or dissociated from history—as in the present instance where the dark tendencies of the human heart are projected onto an alien personality.

American literature broadly conceived from Colonial times on reveals only one notable early instance of the demon as *persona* in Michael Wigglesworth's poetic apocalypse *The Day of Doom*, which Perry Miller somewhat facetiously designated the "first bestseller in the annals of the American book trade." [9] Even a detailed survey of the last two formative centuries of our literature seems to confirm Scott's judgment at least so far as the demonic *figura* is concerned. Again, only one instance of the demonic *persona* stands

out—the Satan in Mark Twain's *The Mysterious Stranger*—but
that characterization is hardly unequivocal. Although Twain's solipsistic revealer calls himself "Satan," he is only Satan's nephew
and an "unfallen angel" at that. Despite this equivocation on Philip
Traum's part, a clear case can be made for considering him a purely
secular avatar of the demon rather than his *figura* in any sense, as
I hope to demonstrate.

The demon as *persona* extrinsic to man is all but absent from
American literature until the present as a literary phenomenon to
be reckoned with; however, human counterparts of the demonic
have played a significant part in American letters. There are two
strands of these American literary variations on the demonic, and
it is only against the background analysis of established trends that
recent developments can be assessed. One strand is retrospective
and its literary analogue of the demonic is privatized; the other is
proleptic, its demonic variation a social phenomenon, though still
basically intrinsic to mankind. The retrospective strand emphasizes
the Edenic source of the demon in man's heart and traces a literary
line from Hawthorne through Nathanael West to Flannery O'Connor; [10] the proleptic strain imagines the mythical end-time of the
last loosing of Satan, yet in terms of the protean presence of the
confidence man. In both strains, the demonic is primarily an image
of man, and hence we are dealing on the literal level with a recognizably human "world of the work." Yet both are, it seems to me,
at least broadly figural in the sense that I have preserved above
(*pace* Scott) inasmuch as the principal works employing human
analogues of the demonic impart a sense of the mystery of evil that
cannot simply be explained as the sum of man's offenses or controlled through merely human efforts.

A standard treatment of the demonic heart is Harry Levin's
The Power of Blackness which explores the dark side of the nineteenth-century imagination as opposed to the official optimism:
"Where the voice of the majority is by definition affirmative, the
spirit of independence is likeliest to manifest itself by employing
the negative: by saying *no* in thunder—as Melville wrote to Hawthorne—though bidden by the devil himself to say *yes*." [11] The
classic though brief analysis of the loosing of Satan image is in
R. W. B. Lewis's essay on the American literary strand of "ludi-
crous catastrophe" from Melville's *The Confidence-Man*, through
Twain's *The Mysterious Stranger* and West's *The Day of the
Locust*, into the present in O'Connor, Ellison, Barth, Pynchon, and

Heller.[12] While happily acknowledging the brilliance of Lewis's seminal insight into this strain, I have tried elsewhere to specify what I would consider to be the theological nuances of this literary tradition.[13]

II

The strain of the demonic heart in seeking to explain man's present predicament looks retrospectively toward the origin of his perversity. Nathaniel Hawthorne is the American master of the romance concerned with exposing the mystery of the demon's lasting influence on the race sprung from Eden's shadows, and the *locus classicus* in his *oeuvre* is doubtlessly the conclusion to "Earth's Holocaust." The prairie conflagration in which men hope to destroy forever the world's "accumulation of wornout trumpery" is actually a travesty of renewal because they have failed to submit to the flame's purification the only possible source of new life. "What but the human heart itself?" insists the "dark-visaged stranger" whose "eyes glowed with a redder light than that of the bonfire." The first-person narrator of the sketch, with authorial precision, acknowledges how sad it is "that man's agelong endeavor for perfection had served only to render him the mockery of the evil principle, from the fatal circumstance of an error at the very root of the matter. The heart, the heart—there was the little yet boundless sphere wherein existed the original wrong of which the crime and misery of this outward world were merely types. Purify that inward sphere, and the many shapes of evil that haunt the outward, and which now seem almost our only realities, will turn to shadowy phantoms and vanish of their own accord."

In another apposite sketch of Hawthorne's, "The Celestial Railroad," Mr. Smooth-it-away, accompanying the narrator on his first trip to the Celestial City, is a perfect caricature of the nineteenth-century optimism which believed that industrialization could cut a sure path to salvation. Seeing him finally for the charlatan he is, the narrator wonders how Mr. Smooth-it-away was able "to deny the existence of Tophet, when he felt its fiery tortures raging within his breast." The man's face reveals the demonic origin of his facile doctrine: "A smoke-wreath issued from his mouth and nostrils, while a twinkle of lurid flame darted out of either eye, proving indubitably that his heart was all of a red blaze."

Hawthorne's "Ethan Brand" describes the tragic fate of a man who roams the world searching for the Unpardonable Sin, never realizing that he carried the secret within himself. In his ruthless intellectual experimentation with another human being, his own heart "had withered—had contracted—had hardened—had perished!" Brand's suicidal leap into a kiln that converts marble into lime reveals the truth about his fiendish heart; "it is burnt into what looks like special good lime." The community experiment in *The Blithedale Romance* aborts because the enduring influence of the demonic Westervelt is more genuine than Zenobia's Edenic masquerade. The wooden head of the magician's walking stick "is carved in vivid imitation of that of a serpent." Coverdale, however, sees Westervelt's smile that reveals false teeth as the mark of his satanic connections: "Every human being, when given over to the devil, is sure to have the wizard mark upon him, in one form or another. I fancied that this smile, with its peculiar revelation, was the devil's signet on the Professor."

A century later in a decidedly more humid climate, a shy Southern girl kept alive the demonic *figura* in American fiction. Although with the passage of time the romance tradition was all but confined to the genre of the grotesque, Flannery O'Connor despite her relatively slight literary output made a substantial contribution to the permanence of traditional Judaeo-Christian symbolism. Although most unbiased estimates of cultural trends have admitted that for mid-twentieth-century America she was definitely singing out of chorus, the volume of critical consideration that she has received recently can readily make one wonder who was on key to begin with.

The presence of the grotesque in Flannery O'Connor is an enduring reminder of man's spiritual deformity, and the origin of that deformity—O'Connor agreed completely with Hawthorne—is our race's brotherhood in sin. The catalogue of O'Connor's explicitly demonic characterizations is impressive: Mr. Paradise in "The River," The Misfit in "A Good Man Is Hard to Find," Powell Boyd in "A Circle in the Fire," Manley Pointer in "Good Country People," Sarah Ham in "The Comforts of Home," Mary Grace in "Revelation," Rufus Johnson in "The Lame Shall Enter First," and the homosexual-rapist in *The Violent Bear It Away*, although there is a cosmic dimension to the latter's development that belongs to the loosing-of-Satan strand.

An interesting variation in O'Connor's portrayal of the demonic heart over Hawthorne lies in the fact that her demonic personalities generally admit their deformity; their diabolical nature does not have to be discovered, as in Hawthorne, only acknowledged. Mr. Paradise with the "purple" cancer over his left ear "favors" one of Mrs. Connin's pigs that has an ear bitten off, but behaves more like the hogs of the Gerasenes after Jesus had driven the demon named "Legion" into them (Mark 5:1–10); "he always comes [to the river] to show he ain't been healed." The fat Bobby Lee reminds June Star "of a pig," a fitting companion to The Misfit who at one minute professes "no pleasure but meanness" since he is convinced Jesus "didn't raise the dead," and the next minute that "it's no real pleasure in life," after decimating three generations of a family. Powell Boyd, whose stare seems to pinch Mrs. Cope "like a pair of tongs," lives an adolescent variation of The Misfit's philosophy of life that one ought to enjoy himself "by killing somebody or burning down his house or doing some other meanness to him." Since he cannot own Mrs. Cope's woods, he and his two juvenile cronies burn them to the ground so that they "would never have to think of it again." The "good country" Bible salesman Manley Pointer proves to the sophisticated Hulga that the demonic heart can be more vicious even than the educated mind; as he leaves with Hulga's artificial leg, her ersatz soul, he assures her, "You ain't so smart. I been believing in nothing ever since I was born."

The simple truth about the demonic that O'Connor affirms is best expressed in the genuine rural wisdom of the Judge, Mrs. McIntyre's first husband, in "The Displaced Person": "The devil you know is better than the devil you don't," an insight that O'Connor's intellectuals like Hulga and Thomas seem least capable of absorbing. Thomas in "The Comforts of Home" mistakes the delinquent Sarah Ham, alias Star Drake, for the real demon, his "ruthless" father, whom he allows to take up a squatting position in his mind. Thomas's distorted sense of values deludes him into feeling that the privacy of his temple has been violated by the Antichrist when the nymphomaniacal Sarah enters his bedroom, while permitting the sanctity of his mind to be ravaged by a conniving father. The scowling psychology major Mary Grace, her face "blue with acne," is a portrayal of the kind of subtle possession that would have made *The Exorcist* so much more successful aesthetically. Armed with her text *Human Development* and triggered by Ruby Turpin's condescending social philosophy, the ugly Wellesley girl has a seizure in the doctor's waiting room—the crooked line that Ruby straightens out in her mind with the perseverance of Job. "The Lame Shall

Enter First" offers a variation on O'Connor's thesis about the demonic heart; namely, that those who know their own demons are infinitely better off than those who don't. What makes the hateful Rufus Johnson superior to Sheppard and the latter a "big tin Jesus" is Rufus's willingness to admit that "Satan has [him] in his power." When the lame Johnson carries off the prey (Sheppard's son Norton) as he has prophesied, Sheppard imagines with compunction that he sees "the clear-eyed Devil, the sounder of hearts, leering at him from the eyes of Johnson."

There are two notable instances of traditional literary variations on the demonic that are apparently figural representations of the demonic heart, but on closer examination of the total context are actually parodies of the traditional figural, Philip Traum in Twain's *The Mysterious Stranger* and Shrike in West's *Miss Lonelyhearts*. Specific descriptive touches make it clear that West intended Shrike's portrait as demonic; like the archfiend in whose "comic" image he has been made, Shrike has chosen Christ as his "particular joke." He has even given Miss Lonelyhearts a piece of white cardboard with a blasphemous parody of the *Anima Christi* on it; it begins: "Soul of Miss L, glorify me." More pointed yet is the diabolical pattern of Shrike's seduction of Miss Lonelyhearts, with a tripartite structure of temptation following Saint Luke's version of the trial of Jesus in the wilderness. In a simple parody of Luke's Gospel, Shrike first encourages Miss Lonelyhearts to give his readers stones rather than bread: "When they ask for bread don't give them crackers as does the Church, and don't, like the State, tell them to eat cake. Explain that man cannot live by bread alone and give them stones. Teach them to pray each morning: 'Give us this day our daily stone.'" Shrike's second attempt, interspersed throughout the narrative, consists in his universal display of principles of order, deluding Miss Lonelyhearts into thinking that they are all potentially his. At the climactic moment of Miss Lonelyhearts's last party, Shrike's third temptation urges him to believe that it is really possible to play God, to save the multitudes through the order in one's own life. Succumbing to this fatal presumption, Miss Lonelyhearts predestines himself to death rather than life. The demonic heart traps all lonely hearts whose despair drives them ironically to the presumptive role of self-appointed savior of men. If West himself shows any preference in his short novel, it is for the cynical wisdom of his satanic comedian; he uses the traditional symbolism only to mock the illusions of religion.

Philip Traum in *The Mysterious Stranger* calls himself Satan, as we noted, but acknowledges that he is actually an unfallen angel, Satan's nephew. That Twain should award the name "Satan" to an unfallen angel is perhaps prophetic of the novella's ultimate message: that the only one who has fallen in our world is the God whom Christians have imagined. As a literal messenger of Twain's enlightment, this unfallen angel functions finally in the destructive role of the loosed Satan inasmuch as his solipsistic apocalypse announces the demise of all reality outside of the self. Twain has used traditional symbolism explicitly to lampoon the figural; Satan tells Theodor, "I am but a dream—your dream, creature of your imagination. . . . I, your poor servant, have revealed you to yourself and set you free. Dream other dreams, and better!" Theodor is, after all, nothing more than "a vagrant thought . . . wandering forlorn among the empty eternities!" *The Mysterious Stranger*, because of the finality of its revelation, is thus more appropriately considered with the secularized strand of the loosed Satan. Twain like West in *Miss Lonelyhearts* establishes the traditional only to deride it.

III

Whereas the strand of the demonic heart seeks the origins of man's present failure in the Edenic covenant with the serpent, the loosing of Satan motif projects the result of man's continuing perversity into a catastrophic future of crisis. Earlier even than Twain's *The Mysterious Stranger* is Melville's masterful literary evocation of the confusion of the end-time in *The Confidence-Man*, undoubtedly the definitive secular variation on the Biblical image of the loosed Satan. Its April Fool's Day trip aboard the *Fidèle*, celebrating the protean existence of the superpromiser, becomes a mythic journey into the darkness latent in mid-nineteenth-century American optimism. The sudden appearance of the deaf-mute, the man in cream-colors, an obvious parody on the advent of a Christ who could not have heard the response to his impracticable doctrine, is followed immediately by the arrival of Black Guinea, the first in a series of *seven* major disguises of the confidence man, each duping the public with his own version of the plea for trust.[14] Melville's careful use of the apocalyptic number of completion for the disguises of his loosed Satan suggests the demise of the American dream. The passengers are either duped by the confidence man or immune to his protestations because they have already capitulated to the demon. In Nathanael West's *The Day of the Locust* the evil age that was to be spawned by the loosing of Satan is already present in the dance of death stimulated by Hollywood's illusion of success. No identifiable character represents Satan; it is the pervasive artificiality of the movie industry itself, and by association of all Southern California, that is the demonic institution of empty promises. The bored mass of "starers" who have come to Hollywood to die become in the premiere riot of the final scene swarming locusts of apocalypse, a mushroom cloud of frustrated dreams detonated by a childish prank.

Ralph Ellison's Reverend Bliss P. Rinehart, whose presence heralds the outbreak of the riot at the end of *Invisible Man*, is a consciously-created spiritual descendant of Melville's confidence man. As self-proclaimed "spiritual technologist," pastor of the "Holy Way Station," he invites the public to join him in the "NEW REVELATION of the OLD-TIME RELIGION," when what he really presages is its last revelation. It is doubtless significant to the structure of the novel and to Ellison's artful anticipation of the end-time that Rinehart seems to be known to everyone but the narrator, who, disguised with dark glasses and white hat to avoid Ras the Destroyer, is constantly mistaken for Rinehart. It is thus that he learns the many disguises of the archdeceiver: "Rine the runner and Rine the gambler and Rine the briber and Rine the lover and Rinehart the Reverend." Rinehart is the elusive face of fraud; he is not the only demon though (there are at least three avatars in each of the novel's three divisions), simply the last and greatest in a long line of hypocritical promisers of a future that persistently eludes the grasp. One by one Ellison lifts the masks of exploitation, exposing the myriad impersonal sources of the invisibility of modern man. Although the novel captures the sense of urgency that we are told will pervade the end-time, it ends on a more positive note than either Melville or West was able to sound, the discovery of an enduring spark of love in man that may possibly survive the chaos of depersonalization.

The stranger in Flannery O'Connor's *The Violent Bear It Away* who dialogues with Tarwater after the death of his great-uncle is actually the inner voice of the boy's demonic heart. It is not perhaps until the stranger is so evidently incarnated in the homosexual-rapist (both are portrayed as wearing panama hats, exuding a sweet odor, and having lavender-to-violet eyes) that it becomes obvious how O'Connor's symbolism has been functioning on two levels from the beginning. Paralleling the interior dialogue between Tarwater and the stranger's voice is the exterior sequence of evil counselors culminating in the man in the "lavender and cream-colored car" who eschews counsel for the actual infliction of evil. The satanic avatars include Meeks, the copper-flue salesman, for whom love is a word only; Rayber, Tarwater's atheist schoolteacher uncle; the man on the park bench "of a generally gray appearance" recommending total independence; and the auto-transit truckdriver, interested only in staying awake. Only when he experiences evil-in-the-flesh is Tarwater chastened enough to be able to purge himself of the memory of the stranger's voice and the woods of the place of his violation. Tarwater averts the personal catastrophe of a life without respect for mystery—offered by the stranger and his avatars from the faithless city of man—in preference for the prophetic violence of that true country "where the silence is never broken except to shout the truth."

John Barth's strained allegory *The End of the Road* employs a nameless Negro doctor with an all-white clientele for studied contrast as his secular counterpart of the loosed Satan. The doctor practices Mythotherapy but never offers his patients the singular insight that would make their role-playing successful; his imagination that theoretically could save serves only to enslave Jacob Horner. Barth projects the loss of world that results from the absence of alternatives; existentialism as an absolute leads "to the terminal," where the novel ends.

Whereas Barth begins with humor and ends with the unexpected and horrifying realism of Rennie's actual death at the doctor's hands during an abortion, Walker Percy maintains a humorously satirical balance throughout his "Adventures of a Bad Catholic at a Time Near the End of the World." The most delightful of American secular variations on satanic activities at the end-time is Art Immelmann in *Love in the Ruins*, "the man from the Rockefeller-Ford-Carnegie foundations who looks like a drug salesman," seeking to fund the development of Thomas More's Qualitative-Quantitive Ontological Lapsometer (MOQUOL). More's device, a "modern stethoscope of the spirit," diagnoses the extremes of angelism and bestialism in the human psyche; More intends his invention to diminish human tensions, not increase them as happens when the lapsometer falls into Immelmann's hands. Recognition of Immelmann's demonic nature proceeds in a comic manner con-

sistent with the tone of the rest of Percy's novel: he arrives unexpectedly amid thunder and lightning; he is of course "a stranger";
he "laughs heartily," but abruptly shifts moods; he "turns white
and falls back a step" when More says "goddamn." His second
appearance is at a urinal next to More's, a suspicious violation of
"the unspoken rules between men for the use of urinals"; More
exclaims, "Speak of the devil." Another curious oddity of Immelmann's, setting him farther apart from the rest of men, is his
perverse habit of "dressing" on the wrong side ("not one American
male in a thousand," ask any tailor, "dresses" on the right). Immelmann's abuse of the lapsometer, aside from increasing psychic
tensions, activates the sulphurous deposits below a suburban golf
course. More must eventually pray to his namesake to be exorcised
of the demon rather than lose his girl friend and presumably his
world: "Sir Thomas More, kinsman, saint, best dearest merriest
of Englishman, pray for us and drive this son of a bitch hence."
Immelmann disappears into the swirling smoke that typifies his
origin and destiny, and the measure of the catastrophe he has created. Be careful what you pretend to do or of the company you
keep (with foundations), Percy warns; we are too often victimized
by our own inventions. Like the best of American apocalyptists,
he painstakingly catalogues our failures, however grievous, in hopes
that the future will realize decidedly better possibilities. The loosed
Satan, therefore, though generally taking individual human shape
even while having universal influence, never represents a source of
evil simply apart from the sins of human institutions at least, although in these broadly figural works it is likewise never a question
of their mere accumulation.

IV

Whatever else one may say about Blatty's adaptation of *The Exorcist* for the screen and Friedkin's direction of it, the film's introduc-
tory sequence in Northern Iraq establishes a cosmic context for
the vulgar Georgetown incident that avoids the novel's almost trite
clinical tone and inconclusive ending. The final shot of that sequence discloses with apocalyptic insistence the ancient enemies
poised for control of the globe, Christ and Satan, as Father Merrin
and the winged demon join battle over the setting sun. However
brilliant the frame, it suggests the facile dualism of Old Testament
apocalypse; the rest of the film does nothing to dispel this impres-

sion inasmuch as good wins out completely in the end, the predictably simplistic solution that commentators favoring prophecy over apocalypse invariably deprecate. The structure of the New Testament Book of Revelation, in my judgment at least, implies the rejection of any facile conclusion to the struggle between Christ and Satan, while maintaining belief in the ultimate victory of Christ.

In contrast with the classically apocalyptic juxtaposition of Father Merrin and the demon, the discovery of Karras's medal in the same Iraqi tell with the ancient demonic figurine is typical of the inanity of all that follows. Are we to conclude that the devil in claiming Karras kept a souvenir (duplicate) of his minor physical victory over a doubting priest? Yet for all Father Karras's problems with faith, his doubt is worth saving infinitely more than Regan's superficial innocence. There is moreover a regrettable Neo-Puritan implication in both the novel and the film that sex is demonic since practically all of Regan's aberrant activities are portrayed in terms of sexual excesses. In fact the only references to sex are aberrations—not the least of *The Exorcist*'s omissions, however. Its most significant and unpardonable is its failure to portray *any* evil in the world camparable to what the demon perpetrates in Regan. Chris MacNeil, Regan's mother, curses up a storm, meriting second place only to the demon, yet there is no indication that we are to take this as anything other than understandable lamentation. And Father Karras suspects that he has lost or is losing his faith, but in the resolution of the conflict makes the supreme practical sacrifice that Christian faith could possibly ask; he gives his troubled life for Regan's freedom.

The Exorcist and similar contemporary phenomena seem without exception to be guilty of man's recurring, culturally primitive tendency to abdicate responsibility for his crimes by making the source of evil external to himself. And for this reason alone the recurrence of the demonic *persona* is aesthetically unjustifiable and intellectually reprehensible. It is, I believe, readily verifiable that primitive religious man placed evil outside himself in nature, in unknown malignant spirits, and that a singular blessing of the world's great religions is their determination to subjectify evil. And although the literary interiorization of evil does not, as I have suggested, necessarily entail the demise of the figural, particularly in the loosing of Satan strain, the return of the demonic *persona* as pure externalization of evil clearly destroys the literal basis of the figural—an added significant reason for denying the form a place in genuine literary history.

If Karl Menninger is correct in his estimate of our current public posture regarding sin,[15] then the return of Satan as literary and cinematic *persona* is simply another confirmation of the modern American abdication of high ethical sensibility in favor of the archaic and the bizarre. The word "sin" is no longer in currency; we would prefer to blame the environment or the government and its institutions, or psychic states that paralyze the will. Even the recent Liberation Theology, however important it may seem to minority self-identity, externalizes evil; although the oppressors are invariably men and their institutions, they are at least by definition external to the oppressed minority.

If the inclination to abdicate personal moral responsibility is indeed the broader cultural tendency that is only gradually affecting the literary and cinematic imagination, we have at least some consolation and perhaps hope in the realization that a stronger voice in American letters is still speaking for the universal demonic heart. John Gardner's *Grendel* (Alfred A. Knopf, 1971), which retells the Beowulf legend from the monster's point of view, happily addresses the very problem unintentionally raised by the purveyors of the Satanic *persona*. Grendel realizes that he is serving as a natural therapy for mankind and it devastates him. The symbols of the demon and the monster are of course intimately related in literary history; it is encouraging to know that another promising young writer—aware of literary tradition—is using the bizarre intelligently.

Interesting analogies can be made, finally, to yet another strand of Western symbolism, the Wild Man. Edward Dudley and Maxmillian E. Novak's fascinating collection of essays, significantly entitled *The Wild Man Within*, traces the development of two variants in this symbolism from the Renaissance to Romanticism that spring from classical discriminants. The Greeks and the Romans perceived the differentiation of the wild man as physical and cultural, the Hebrews and Christians as moral and metaphysical.[16] The former tended to objectify, or physicalize, what the latter called internal, spiritual, or psychological—a distinction with patent similarities to my estimate of the return of Satan in relation to established strands of the demonic in American literature. The authors' concluding observations are worth relating to the subject at hand: "The Wild Man, along with all the other demonic forces of nature, has been officially demythologized. He is merely those energies which have previously evaded the organizing forces of the City of God or the City of Man. But in spite of his demythologization, the Wild Man has successfully resisted encroachments on his domain. Science has only managed a few exploratory probings and some tentative control measures. Even Carl Jung, the most optimistic of searchers, has declared the unconscious uneducable, and so the future of wildness seems assured. . . . We can learn to live with wildness and its burning energy only if we redeem ourselves. The question is still redemption or tragic destruction." [17] We shall have saved ourselves from tragic self-destruction, I would add, only if we can accept the demonic *within ourselves* and the institutions we have made—and our need for redemption.

NOTES

1. "Background Material on *The Exorcist*" (Burbank, Calif.: Warner Bros., 1973), p. 2.
2. *Ibid.*
3. *The New Yorker*, January 7, 1974.
4. *The New York Times*, December 27, 1973.
5. Gerard Manley Hopkins, "God's Grandeur."
6. Other less successful and also apparently less widely read novels, appealing to the demonic and made into films, are John Buell's *Pyx* (1970) and Ramona Stewart's *The Possession of Joel Delaney* (1970). Recent plays worth considering in a broader cultural context, all employing the demonic but in varying degrees, include Arthur Miller's *The Crucible* (1953), Robert Marasco's *Child's Play* (1970), Edward Albee's *Who's Afraid of Virginia Woolf?*, Act II, "Walpurgisnacht" (1962), and Howard Richardson and William Berney's *Dark of the Moon* (1973). The first three of course gained additional cultural exposure through their film adaptations.
7. Nathan A. Scott, Jr., *The Wild Prayer of Longing: Poetry and the Sacred* (New Haven: Yale University Press, 1971), p. 25.
8. Erich Auerbach, *Mimesis: The Representation of Reality in Western Literature* (Princeton: Princeton University Press, 1953).
9. Perry Miller, *Errand Into the Wilderness* (New York: Harper & Row, 1964), p. 218.
10. Although Poe's imagination falls decidedly to the side of darkness and a case could perhaps be made for treating stories like "The Cask of Amontillado," "The Tell-Tale Heart," and "The Pit and the Pendulum" as studies in the demonic heart, I prefer to see Poe as more closely related to the genre of horror and the macabre that in Harry Levin's words "prefers to dwell upon the psychology of crime rather than upon the ethics of guilt" (*The Power of Blackness*, p. 122). My concern here is with writers who make more obvious moral judgments about man and his world, and not

even with those existential and psychological horrors linked with the human condition.

11. Harry Levin, *The Power of Blackness* (New York: Vintage Books, 1969), p. 7.

12. R. W. B. Lewis, "Days of Wrath and Laughter," in *Trials of the Word* (New Haven: Yale University Press, 1965), pp. 184–235.

13. *Cf.* my *Toward a New Earth: Apocalypse in the American Novel* (Notre Dame, Indiana: University of Notre Dame Press, 1972), especially pages 209 to 220. What Lewis treats under the broad general rubric of humorous apocalypse can, I feel, be further distinguished from a religious perspective as antichristian and secular, the latter category including apocalypse of despair as well as humorous apocalypse taken in a narrow sense. It is my thesis that humorous apocalypse is the most recent but hopeful variation of the loosing of Satan motif to appear since the conscious demythologizing literary efforts of Twain and West; for if one carefully distinguishes the humor in recent literary apocalypse from "black humor" it seems quite feasible to read Ellison, Pynchon, Vonnegut, Heller and even some of Barth as the imaginative protestations of men who care enough to envision the very worst, but as a deterrent to catastrophe, not an announcement of it.

14. *Ibid.*, pp. 62–72.

15. Karl A. Menninger, *Whatever Became of Sin?* (New York: Hawthorn Books, Inc., 1973).

16. Edward Dudley and Maxmillian E. Novak, eds., *The Wild Man Within: An Image in Western Thought from the Renaissance to Romanticism* (University of Pittsburgh Press, 1972), pp. 10–11.

17. *Ibid.*, pp. 312–13.

Erazim V. Kohák

SPEAKING OF THE DEVIL: A MODEST METHODOLOGICAL PROPOSAL

I *The Matter of Existence*

SPEAKING OF THE DEVIL, as we do in this volume, poses some unique methodological problems. If we were to believe the devil exists, we would be well advised not to speak of him at all. On this point, ageless folk wisdom is virtually unanimous. It warns us repeatedly that if we take the devil's name in vain, he just might materialize on the spot, to our regret. The less said, the better: the devil, it seems, likes his privacy. In Czech folklore the warning is specific: "Nemaluj čerta na zed!" ("Don't paint the devil on the wall!") The English injunction is more consistent. It avoids all explicit mention and just warns us, "Don't even think about it." If in face of all such warnings we still propose to speak of the devil, it might be far safer if we assume from the start that the devil does not exist.

But the devil of this is that once we deny the devil's existence, we have effectively precluded all possibility of access to empirical information about him. If the devil does not exist, there simply is nothing to say. We might still be able to concoct charming tales in which we attribute all our pet dislikes to the devil. C. S. Lewis, in his altogether delightful *Screwtape Letters*, assures us, for instance, that the devil finds evangelical denominations far less offensive than high Anglican Church. He may well be right, but that assertion can hardly be considered hard, empirical datum. Lewis himself, in *The Great Divorce*, refrains from any mention of the devil, altogether confident that humans are quite capable of staffing hell unaided. But there is the rub: if we affirm the devil's existence, we

48

had better not speak of him; while if we deny it, there is nothing to be said. Damned if we do and damned if we don't—the antinomies of the devil's existence block all fruitful inquiry at the start.

For that reason I propose to adopt a methodology which differs significantly from the wonted ways of both natural and human sciences and approach the question phenomenologically. For the moment I will suspend the question of whether the devil does or does not exist. Perhaps he does, perhaps he does not: I will leave the matter in brackets. What will concern us instead is how the *eidos* or *type* of experience which we associate with the word "devil" functions in the context of human life: what, if you wish, it means to speak of the devil.

Let me emphasize: our topic will be the *eidos* "devil"—not the "idea." The idea, including all speculations about the devil from Jean Wier's *De Praestigiis Daemonium* to Denis de Rougemont's *The Devil's Share*, shall remain suspended. It will remain, of course, as datum in the experience of all who have read either book, but, like the existence or nonexistence of the devil, the idea of the devil shall have no privileged explanatory status in our investigations. I am concerned solely with devil-experience—with the way the *eidos* "devil" functions in the economy of ordinary life. In sum, I will not inquire into theories about the devil, nor into his existence or nonexistence, but solely into that particular type of experience which the word "devil" indicates.

11 The Devil Among Us

Information about the *eidos* devil—the devil experience in daily life—is by far most readily available in the folklore of nations passing through the final stages of feudalism into the first stages of industrialization. Not that the experience was absent in pre-industrial society: quite the contrary. But there its expression remains clouded and inarticulate, largely locked in cryptic dicta and obscure customs. Before we can decode them, we need to find a more articulate model as a guide. Early industrialization, with its demand for written articulation, provides that. Quite simply, fairy tales are still told, but they are also being written down.

On the other side, it is definitely not the case that the devil experience ceases with the industrial revolution. Far from it. But industrialization obscures it once again, this time by inserting a layer of tools between the subject and his world. The devil experience, though no less real, is now far more readily symbolized in terms of mechanical malfunction of that intermediate level. The subject is likely to explain missing a crucial appointment by saying that for some (damned?) reason his (damned?) car just would not start, rather than by blaming the devil directly and accusing him of possessing his horse. Infernal machines simply become more available than devilish machinations for purposes of symbolizing the experience of evil.

One must, therefore, turn to the folklore of late feudalism, as recorded during the early stages of industrialization, for there the devil does assume a reasonably definite shape. It is not the familiar shape: the red union suit with an "H" (which, allegedly at least, does not stand for "Harvard") is a late Western invention. The traditional devil of folklore appears more often in the guise of a swarthy forester, usually clubfooted (betraying his kinship with the once and future god Pan). Half man, half goat, the devil of folklore conjures up the unchained, pre-ethical dimension of human experience, of impulse and instinct. Since humans have chosen the path of social responsibility, that affinity now appears disruptive, but it is real nonetheless. The things the devil does are frequently things which humans "wouldn't dream of doing"—but, though properly shocked, are not altogether displeased to have someone do for or to them. The explanation that "the devil made me do it" was not always a joke. Its full intent is double: "Thank the devil, he made me do it: I wouldn't have dared otherwise," but also "Thank God *the devil* made me do it: now no one can blame me." In a classic instance, the devil drives a farmer out of town by giving him all the things he wants—stolen openly from his neighbors.[1] In this version, the devil of folklore essentially exploits suppressed aspects of being human as well as human weakness and affirms a certain rightness of things: inordinate desire will not be denied, but it will also not be unpunished.

In a second version, the devil of folklore appears rather less humanoid. The *šetek* or *raráš* in the tales collected by Erben [2] is a four-legged creature sporting a coxcomb and chicken claws on its hind legs. It is capricious rather than vicious, capable of bringing both good fortune and ill, for no apparent reason. It might change a poor farmer's fortune by killing his horses and turning the hides into a sleek, powerful team, or it might set his roof on fire. Here the devil of folklore reflects the capriciousness of all human experience, the fickleness of fortune.

A third version presents the devil as openly malicious. That devil lurks in all the interstices of human life as a destructive agent kept at bay only by unceasing vigilance. Life is a contest with him, to be won by effort, care or guile. Here the devil symbolizes the same experience as the English dictum, "If something can go wrong, it will." It is not a matter of human weakness nor of the fickleness of fortune, but of what appears almost an innate tendency of things to deteriorate.

But in all three masks, as tempter, trickster or spoiler, the devil of folklore is not basically demonic. The devil, as folklore presents him, is still natural—he belongs. He is a part of life, perhaps an unfortunate, upsetting or threatening part of life, but still a part of it. The relationship to humans is by no means onesided, as in the story recorded by Němcová.[3] Here the devil plays on a woman's pride, only to find himself stuck with the marriage-hungry Káča clinging to his back. A shepherd frees him by taking his coat, Káča and all, and dumping it in a millpond. The devil repays the shepherd by letting him ostensibly save two noblemen from hell for rich reward, while the shepherd in turn tricks the devil, saving a third man by threatening the devil with Káča. The relationship is one of give and take, and in some stories becomes even symbiotic. Even when it does not, there are always remedies and precautions to keep the devil within bounds. The devil of folklore thus does not upset the system—he belongs to it as trouble belongs to human life. There is misfortune which must be simply counted as a part of "the way life is," there is misfortune which is the price of great fortune, and there is misfortunte rooted in the perennial conflict of freedom and security. The devil figure of folklore articulates all of them. It is as much a part of the human lot as they are—the hard part, the unpredictable part, the unfortunate part—yes, but still a part of life.

Folklore recognizes this in the strategies it adopts in dealing with the devil. Essentially, they are prudential strategies, less a matter of opposing a great good force to a great evil force than a matter of taking some fairly commonsensical precautions against the hazards of living. Against the danger of internal conflict, folklore prescribes various forms of mental hygiene, against the exorbitant price of inordinate desire, moderation; and against the irrational misfortunes of daily existence, a set of equally irrational daily precautions: setting out with the right foot, wearing a lucky charm, bewaring the Ides of March (or Friday the 13th), knocking on wood (for the curious: three knocks—the Morse letter *S*—from below, on unvarnished surface, are most effective). The rule, "Praise God but don't offend the devil," is quite apt here. Altogether, the devil of folklore is, by and large, *bad,* but not really *demonic.*

III *Intimations of the Demonic*

Folklore remedies for evil, however, also include an altogether different category. Unlike the rather matter-of-fact remedies for the devil, these are without exception awesome, awe-full invocations of great power: the sign of the cross, the Body and Blood of Christ, prayer and exorcism—or their non-ecclesiastical equivalents, invocations of great gods whom the Church has long forgotten. These are no longer home remedies applicable to the devil in, so to speak, man-to-man dealings. They are the ultimate resort of humans confronted with a radically life-destroying evil which is truly demonic and can no longer be contained within the system, but must be countered by a plea for a saving grace which is also an admission of human helplessness.

The forces against which such remedies are involked are no longer "natural," as the devil of ordinary folklore who is very much a part of "the way the ball bounces." They are *radically* evil, rejoicing in destruction. For all the ills flesh is heir to, there is no such evil in nature. Nature includes tough luck; radical evil stems from human intent. In older categories, we could say that while playing with the devil of folklore we are dealing with a mask of "natural" evil, here we encounter *historical* evil, evil in history rather than nature.

Perhaps the most striking trait of such evil—reflected in folklore in tales of vampires, werewolves and the undead—is its utter lack of kinship with nature. Its basic kinship is with the human. While the devil of folklore was still basically a natural force, the vampire and the werewolf are perversions of human intent. They are in fact humans, but humans radically perverted in their humanity, not unfortunate aspects of the natural. And with good reason, for only the human capable of great good is also capable of radical evil, of a conscious, purposeful perversion and negation of the good. Immanuel Kant recognized that only a good will can be radically good. Folklore recognizes the hidden obverse: only an evil will can be radically evil.

Human experience gives that recognition a powerful meaning. Animals prey on each other (though they are also capable of symbiosis)—that is just the way it is. But where in nature could we find something as monstrous, as radically evil, as the will which sent endless lines of emaciated, naked human beings threading into gas chambers—humans who were once workers and professors, wives and musicians, who loved and were loved? Where in nature can we find an analogue to the will which set armies marching into Czechoslovakia on 21 August 1968 to break the hearts, hopes and lives of two nations? The pall of smoke over Oswiecim, the pall of words that kill all life over Czechoslovakia, lack all metaphors in nature: that is evil whose masks are no longer those of the devil, but of *the demonic*.

Folklore recognizes another significant aspect of the demonic. It is not only a perversion of will, but it is most often a perversion of great good will. In fairy tales, it is usually great love thwarted which creates the hate that lives beyond the grave. "Hell," we are told, "has no fury like a woman scorned!" Of course not. It takes the power of great love to fuel a great hate. Czech peasants used to make the sign of the cross against a Jesuit. Yet the force that kindled the fires of the Inquisition and reconverted Bohemia to Catholicism at the cost of its soul and two-thirds of its population did not start out as petty malice, but as great dedication, great devotion to a great ideal. Ignatius Loyola is a saint. Even Lenin did not *set out* to build a prison of souls and bodies: he too set out to make men holy—in a Marxist interpretation of the word, to be sure, but holy all the same. The great evil he bequeathed to Stalin and his successors is the fruit of great good thwarted.

That evil is not unambiguous. Count Dracula, the Roumanian national hero who defended his people with an iron hand against their enemies and with the same iron hand gave them a stable order amid the chaos which ground humans to cinders in surrounding countries, could become the "Dracula" of fiction because to Bram Stoker's Magyar informers a Roumanian hero appeared as the incarnation of evil. Even Stalin appears less an incarnation of evil will to Russians and Georgians than to Estonians, Latvians, Lithuanians, Poles, Czechs, Slovaks and other non-Russian victims of Russian imperialism. Had Hitler won the war, German estimation of him today might be less compatible with the Dutch, the Polish or the Czech.

To be sure, not all great love, not even great love thwarted, produces great hate. Folklore includes examples of love that lives— the fallen hero who watches over his people like King Ječmínek in

Moravian lore, or the princess whose ghost watches out of a ruined tower for her beloved and blesses the young lovers below. The love which turns to hate already has certain characteristics of hate. Arrogance is one: it is the lover who would rather see his beloved dead than happy in another's arms who will become a vampire. Self-righteousness is another: it is the idealist so convinced of his righteousness that he sees dissent as vice and all means as holy in his service who will become the Torquemada. It is love without humility which turns to hate.

In all this, there is a common trait: While there is misfortune, even tragic misfortune in nature, radical evil comes into the world through human will. This devil is a fallen angel.

IV *Renouncing the Devil*

What we have said so far provides little to feed the silly fashion of satanism. Silly it is: believing, conjuring or exorcising the devil made sense only in an age which still experienced the devil as the presence of evil, not its mask merely. Since to our age the devil is a mask rather than an incarnation, we need to deal with the reality which the mask reveals rather than with the mask.

Whether or not a devil "exists" as the causal agent behind human misfortune, still, in human experience, that misfortune wears two basic masks: the mask of the devil of folklore and the mask of the demonic. The mask of the devil of folklore reflects the intrinsic contradictions of human existence: the conflict of the longing for security and the surge of freedom, the inordinate price of inordinate desire, the irrational dumb bad luck which is part and parcel of being human. The devil who can be domesticated as a part of life is the devil against whom ordinary remedies—as "natural" as the devil himself—can be effective.

The mask of the demonic is another matter. It reveals the possibilities for destruction inherent in human freedom. It is the mask of a will which, because it can be good, can also be endlessly evil. Against the demonic, home remedies do not avail. The "natural," domesticated devil could be handled with home remedies because he represented the negation of *parts* of a system—in this case, of human life. He may stop a cow's milk, punish a miser or carry off a lecher, but he functions within the system, must play by its rules, and so can be countered by its rules. Rather paradoxically, the devil of folklore can be said to be reasonable: he can be deprived of opportunities, offered compensation, or thwarted by prevention. The demonic is basically different. It is not negation within the system, but a self-negation of the system in its entirety. It is a basic perversion of human will to live, taking the human freedom to create and perverting it into the freedom to humiliate, soil and destroy. The demonic cannot be deprived of opportunities. Though its overt target may be some particular aspect of the human situation, changing that will not help. The intent to destroy can find another target. Nor can it be offered compensation: since it is a basic negation of human potential, it cannot be bribed—it wishes to destroy even the bribe itself. As in the case of Hitler gloating over the destruction of Germany to the bitter end, *Götterdämerung* is its triumph. It cannot be thwarted by prevention: prevention does not make evil impossible, only more costly—and if destruction is the aim, the cost does not matter. The demonic will-to-evil can only be countered by an equally resolute will-to-good: by a consistent affirmation of the life which the demonic negates.

Peasants know the difference, hanging horseshoes on the barn (open end up, please—otherwise the good luck will flow out) to bar access to the devil, but making the sign of the cross against the evil eye. The Church has been less clear: it has a clear conception of the demonic—the devil as fallen angel, "sin" coming into the world through man, and a series of similar assertions—but it has little conception of the "natural" devil. Christianity, after all, is a historical rather than a natural religion. Believers have frequently filled the gap by baptizing traditional remedies for bad luck into Christ by placing them in the charge of particular saints. But all too often the Church has appeased the demonic as if it were merely unfortunate, while invoking the power of God and anathematizing the unfortunate as demonic.

In social philosophy the difference is perhaps most striking and least recognized. There is a basic difference in kind between the fortuitous, unintended ill men do to each other in the process of social existence and the evil of perverted idealism. It need not be a difference in quantity: it would be hard to judge whether the fortuitous suffering with which Europe paid for its industrial revolution was quantitatively more or less than the suffering imposed by the Counter Reformation in Bohemia or by more recent attempts to make men holy. But there is a basic difference in kind. The first is still amenable to natural remedies—changing political rules governing the economy, growth of labor unions, democratization of political and economic processes, persistent defense of human freedom. The second represents a radical negation of humanity: Hitlerism or Stalinism is not amenable to home remedies. It has to be countered by an equally resolute affirmation of freedom and social justice. Lenin's revolution taught us what happens if we try to cope with natural evil (here capitalism in early industrialization) as if it were demonic. Munich taught us no less clearly what happens if we treat the demonic as if it were domesticable.

V But Does the Devil Exist?

The question concerning the devil's "existence" seems to be, therefore, rather spurious. But is it? The devil, after all, is omnipresent. All human *being* and *doing* in the world is marked by contradiction and plain hard luck, and human will is capable both of realization and of perversion. We cannot avoid seeing it—unless, of course, we become convinced that the devil can be located, that he exists here or there, particular rather than ubiquitous. Once we no longer see the devil as a mask of evil but as a "force" or a "person," we can concentrate on "fighting the devil," and ignore the reality of evil, as the social-action record of denominations most committed to "believing in the devil" attests.

Denis de Rougemont opens his book with a sentence from Baudelaire: "The Devil's cleverest wile is to convince us that he does not exist." [4] With all due respect, I beg to differ. The Devil's cleverest wile, I submit, is precisely to convince us that he exists.

NOTES

1. Jaromír Erben, *České pohádky* (Prague: SNDK, 1964), pp. 140–143.
2. *Ibid.*, p. 154.
3. Božena Němcová, *Zlatá kniha pohádek* (Olomouc: Promberger, 1946), pp. 233–241.
4. Denis de Rougemont *The Devil's Share*. Trans. Haakon Chevalier (Washington, D.C.: Bollingen, 1944, 1952), p. 17. In fairness to de Rougemont, whose book is easily the most perceptive treatment of the topic, he recognizes "particularity" as the devil's second ruse! *Cf.* pp. 57ff.

Ananda K. Coomaraswamy

WHO IS SATAN AND WHERE IS HELL?

"He that doeth sin is of the Devil"
I John 3:8

THAT IN THIS day and age, when "for most people religion has
become an archaic and impossible refuge," [1] men no longer take
either god or Satan seriously, arises from the fact that they have
come to think of both alike only objectively, only as persons external to themselves and for whose existence no adequate proof can
be found. The same, of course, applies to the notions of their respective realms, heaven and hell, thought of as times and places
neither now nor here.

We have, in fact, ourselves postponed the "kingdom of heaven
on earth" by thinking of it as a material Utopia to be realized, we
fondly hope, by means of one or more five-year plans, overlooking
the fact that the concept of an endless progress is that of a pursuit
"in which thou must sweat eternally," [2] a phrase suggestive less
of heaven than of hell. What this really means is that we have
chosen to substitute a present hell for a future heaven we shall
never know.

The doctrine to be faced, however, is that "the kingdom of
heaven is within you" here and now, and that, as Jacob Boehme,
amongst others, so often said, "heaven and hell are everywhere,
being universally extended. . . . Thou are accordingly in heaven or
hell. . . . The soul hath heaven or hell within itself," [3] and cannot
be said to "go to" either when the body dies. Here, perhaps, the
solution of the problem of Satan may be sought.

It has been recognized that the notion of a Satanic "person," the chief of many "fallen Angels," presents some difficulties: even in religion, that of a Manichean "dualism" emerges; at the same time, if it be maintained that anything whatever is not God, God's infinity is thereby circumscribed and limited. Is "he" (Satan) then a person, or merely a "personification," *i.e.*, postulated personality? [4] Who is "he" and where? Is he a serpent or a dragon, or has he horns and a poisonous tail? Can he be redeemed and regenerated, as Origen and the Muslims have believed? All these problems hang together.

However the ultimate truth of "dualism" may be repudiated, a kind of dualism is logically unavoidable for all practical purposes, because any world in time and space, or that could be described in words or by mathematical symbols, must be one of contraries, both quantitative and qualitative, for example, long and short, good and evil; and even if it could be otherwise, a world without these opposites would be one from which all possibility of choice, and of procedure from potentiality to act, would be excluded, not a world that could be inhabited by human beings such as we. For anyone who holds that "God made the world," the question, "Why" did He permit the existence in it of any evil, or that of the Evil One in whom all evil is personified, is altogether meaningless; one might as well inquire why He did not make a world without dimensions or one without temporal succession.

Our whole metaphysical tradition, Christian and other, maintains that "there are two in us," [5] this man and the Man in this man; and that this is so is still a part and parcel of our spoken language in which, for example, the expression "self-control" implies that there is one that controls and another subject to control, for we know that "nothing acts upon itself," [6] though we forget it when we talk about "self-government." [7] Of these two "selves," outer and inner man, psycho-physical "personality" and very Person, the human composite of body, soul and spirit is built up. Of these two, on the one hand body-and-soul (or mind), and the other, spirit; one is mutable and mortal, the other constant and immortal; one "becomes," the other "is," and the existence of that one that is not, but becomes, is precisely a "personification" or "postulation," since we cannot say of anything that never remains the same that "it is." And however necessary it may be to say "I" and "mine" for the practical purposes of everyday life, our Ego in fact is nothing but a name for what is really only a sequence of observed behaviours.[8]

Body, soul and spirit: can one or the other of these be equated with the Devil? Not the body, certainly, for the body in itself is neither good nor evil, but only an instrument or means to good or evil. Nor the Spirit-intellect, synteresis, conscience, *Agathos Daimon*—for this is, by hypothesis, man's best and most divine part, in itself incapable of error, and our only means of participation in the life and the perfection that is God himself. There remains only the "soul"; that soul which all must "hate" who would be Christ's disciples and which, as Saint Paul reminds us, the Word of God like a two-edged sword "severs from the spirit"; a soul which Saint Paul must have "lost" to be able to say truly that "I live, yet not I, but Christ in me," announcing, like Manṣūr, his own theosis.

Of the two in us, one the "spark" of Intellect or Spirit, and the other Feeling or Mentality, subject to persuasion, it is obvious that the latter is the "tempter," or more truly "temptress." There is in each of us, in this man and that woman alike, an *anima* and *animus*, relatively feminine and masculine *;[9] and, as Adam rightly said, "the woman gave, and I did eat"; also, be it noted, the "serpent," by whom the woman herself was first beguiled, wears, in art, a woman's face. But to avoid all possibility of misunderstanding here, it must be emphasized that all this has nothing whatever to do with a supposed inferiority of women or superiority of men: in this functional and psychological sense any given woman may be "manly" (heroic) or any given man "effeminate" (cowardly).[10]

One knows, of course, that "soul," like "self," is an ambiguous term, and that, in some contexts, it may denote the Spirit or "Soul *of* the soul," or "Self *of* the self," both of which are expressions in common use. But we are speaking here of the mutable "soul" as distinguished from the "spirit," and should not overlook to what extent this *nefesh*, the *anima* after which the human and other "animals" are so called, is constantly disparaged in the Bible,[11] as is the corresponding *nafs* in Islam. This soul is the self to be "denied" (the Greek original meaning "utterly reject," with ontological rather than a merely ethical application), the soul that must be "lost" if "it" is to be saved; and which as Meister Eckhart and the

---

* Those involved with the modern "Women's Movement" will find Coomaraswamy's comments on the traditionally misunderstood relationship between the "feminine" and the "demonic" of special interest in this essay. *Cf.* also "Notes." EDITOR.

Sufis so often say, must "put itself to death," or, as the Hindus and Buddhists say, must be "conquered" or "tamed," for "that is not my Self." This soul, subject to persuasion, and distracted by its likes and dislikes, this "mind" that we mean when we speak of having been "minded to do this or that," is "that which thou callest 'I' or 'myself,'" and which Jacob Boehme thus distinguishes from the I that *is*, when he says, with reference to his own illuminations, that "not I, the I that I am, knows these things, but God in me." We cannot treat the doctrine of the Ego at length, but will only say that, as for Meister Eckhart and the Sufis, "Ego, the word I, is proper to none but God in his sameness," and that "I" can only rightly be attributed to Him and to the one who, being "joined unto the Lord, is one spirit."

That the soul herself, our "I" or "self" itself, should be the Devil, whom we call the "enemy," "adversary," "tempter," "dragon" —never by a personal name[12]—may seem startling, but it is very far from being a novel proposition. As we go on, it will be found that an equation of the soul with Satan has often been enunciated, and that it provides us with an almost perfect solution of all the problems that the latter's "personality" poses. Both are "real" enough for all pragmatic purposes here, in the active life where "evil" must be contended with, and the dualism of the contraries cannot be evaded; but they are no more "principles," no more really real, than the darkness that is nothing but the privation of light.

No one will deny that the battleground on which the psychomachy must be fought out to a finish is within you, or that, where Christ fights, there also must be his enemy, the Antichrist be found. Neither will anyone, "superstition" apart, be likely to pretend that the Temptations of Saint Anthony, as depicted in art, can be regarded otherwise than as "projections" of interior tensions. In the same way that Picasso's "Guernica" is the mirror of Europe's disintegrated soul, "the hell of modern existence," the Devil's horns and sting are an image of the most evil beast in man himself. Often enough it has been said by the "Never-enough honoured Auncients," as well as by modern authors, that "man is his own worst enemy." On the other hand, the best gift for which a man might pray is to be "at peace with himself," [13] and, indeed, for so long as he is not at peace with Himself,[14] he can hardly be at peace with anybody else, but will "project" his own disorders, making of "the enemy"—for example, Germany, or Russia, or the Jews—his "devil." "From whence come wars and fightings among you? Come they not hence, even from your lusts (pleasure, or desires, Skr. kāmāḥ) that contend in your members?" (James 4:1).

As Jung so penetratingly observes: "When the fate of Europe carried into a four-year war of stupendous horror—a war that no one wanted—hardly anyone asked who had caused the war and its continuation." [15] The answer would have been unwelcome: it was "I"—your "I" and mine. For, in the words of another modern psychologist, E. E. Hadley, "the tragedy of this delusion of individuality is that it leads to isolation, fear, paranoid suspicion, and wholly unnecessary hatreds." [16]

All this has always been familiar to the theologians, in whose writings Satan is so often referred to as simply "the enemy." For example, William Law: "You are under the power of no other enemy, are held in no other captivity, and want no other deliverance but from the power of your own earthly self. This is the one murderer of the divine life within you. It is your own Cain that murders your own Abel," [17] and "self is the root, the tree, and the branches of all the evils of our fallen state . . . Satan, or which is the same thing, self-exaltation. . . . This is that full-born natural self that must be pulled out of the heart and *totally* denied, or there can be no disciple of Christ." If, indeed, "the kingdom of heaven is within you," then also the "war in heaven" will be there until Satan has been overcome—that is, until the Man in this man is "master of himself," *selbes gewaltic,* ἐγκρατὴς ἑαυτοῦ.

For the *Theologica Germanica* (chs. 3, 22, 49), it was the Devil's "I, Me, and Mine" that were the cause of his fall. . . . For the self, the I, the me and the like all belong to the Evil Spirit. Behold one or two words can utter all that has been said by these many words: "Be simply and wholly bereft of self." For "there is nothing else in hell, but self-will; and if there were no self-will, there would be no devil and no hell." So, too, Jacob Boehme: "this vile self-hood possesses the world and worldly things; and dwells also in itself, which is dwelling in hell"; and Angelus Silesius:

Nichts anders stürzet dich in Höllenschlund hinein
Als dass verhasste Wort (merk's wohl!): das Mein und Dein.[18]

Nothing throws you down into the jaws of Hell
like the hateful word (mind you!): mine and thine.

(Trans. by Ed.)

Hence the resolve, expressed in a Shaker hymn:

But now from my forehehad I'll quickly erase   5
The stamp of the Devil's great "I." [19]

Citations of this kind could be indefinitely multiplied, all to the effect that of all evil beasts, "the most evil beast we carry in our bosom," [20] "our most godless and despicable part" and "multifarious beast," which our "Inner Man," like a lion tamer, must keep under his control or else will have to follow where it leads.[21] Even more explicit sayings can be cited from Ṣūfī sources, where the soul (*nafs*) is distinguished from the intellect or spirit ('aql, rūḥ) as the Psyche is distinguished from the Pneuma by Philo and in the New Testament, and as *anima* from *animus* by William of Thierry.[22] For the encyclopaedic *Kashfu'l Mahjūb*, the soul is the "tempter," and the type of hell in this world.[23] Al-Ghazālī, perhaps the greatest of the Muslim theologians, calls the soul "the greatest of your enemies"; and more than that could hardly be said of Satan himself. Abū Sā'īd asks: "What is evil, and what is the worst evil?" and answers, "Evil is 'thou,' and the worst evil 'thou' if thou knowest it not"; he, therefore, called himself a "Nobody," refusing, like the Buddha, to identify himself with any namable "personality." [24] Jalālu'd Dīn Rūmī, in his *Mathnawī*, repeats that man's greatest enemy is himself: "This soul," he says, "is hell," and he bids us "slay the soul." "The Soul and *Shaitān* are both one being, but take two forms; essentially one from the first, he became the enemy and envier of Adam," and, in the same way, "the Angel (Spirit) and the Intellect, Adam's helpers, are of one origin but assume two forms." The quarrel of the sensitive soul with the Intellect is like that of a woman with the master of the house. The Ego holds its head high: "decapitation means, to slay the soul and quench its fire in the Holy War" (jihād); and well for him who wins this battle, for "whoever is at war with himself for God's sake, . . . his light opposing his darkness, the sun of his spirit shall never set." [25]

'Tis the fight which Christ,
With his internal Love and Light,
Maintains within man's nature, to dispel
God's Anger, Satan, Sin and Death, and Hell;
The human Self, or Serpent, to devour,
And raise an Angel from it by His Pow'r.
          —JOHN BYROM

"Spark of the soul . . . image of God, that there is ever in all wise at war with all that is not godly . . . and is called the Synderesis" [26] (Meister Eckhart, Pfeiffer, p. 113). "We know that the Law is of the Spirit . . . but I see another law in my members, warring against the Law of the Intellect, and bringing me into captivity. . . . With the Intellect I myself serve the Law of God; but with the flesh the law of sin. . . . Submit yourselves therefore to God: resist the Devil." [27] And similarly in other Scriptures, notably the *Bhagavad Gītā* (6.5, 6): "Lift up the self by the Self, let not self sit back. For, verily, the Self is both the friend and the foe of the self; the friend of one whose self has been conquered by the Self, but to one whose self hath not (been overcome), the Self at war, forsooth, acts as an enemy"; and the Buddhist *Dhammapada* (103, 160, 380), where "the Self is the Lord of the self" and one should "by the Self incite the self, and by the Self gentle self" (as a horse is "broken in" by a skilled trainer), and "one who has conquered self is the best of all champions." (*Cf.* Philostratus, *Vit. Ap.*, 1–13: "Just as we break in skittish and unruly horses by stroking and patting them.")

At the same time, it must not be forgotten that the Psychomachy is also a "battle of love," and that Christ—to whom "ye should be married . . . that we should bring fruit unto God" (Romans 7:3) —already loved the unregenerate soul "in all her baseness and foulness," [28] or that it is of her that Donne says: "Nor ever chaste, except *Thou* ravish me." It was for nothing but "to go and fetch his Lady, whom his Father had eternally given him to wife, and to restore her to her former high estate that the Son proceeded out of the Most High" (Meister Eckhart).[29] The Deity's lance or thunderbolt is, at the same time, his yard, with which he pierces his mortal Bride. The story of the thunder-smitten Semele reminds us that the Theotokos, in the last analysis Psyche, has ever been of Lunar, never herself of Solar stock; and all this is the sum and substance of every "solar myth," the theme of the *Liebesgeschichte Himmels* (Romance of the Heavens) and of the *Drachenkämpfe* (Struggle with the Dragon).

"Heaven and earth: let them be wed again." [30] Their marriage, consummated in the heart, is the *Hieros Gamos, Daivam Mithunam*,[31] and those in whom it has been perfected are no longer anyone, but as He is "who never became anyone." [32] Plotinus' words: "Love is of the very nature of the Psyche, and hence the constant yoking of Eros with the Psyches in the pictures and the myths" [33] might as well have been said of half the world's fairy tales, and especially of the Indian "pictures and myths" of Srī Krishna and the Milkmaids, of which the Indian commentators rightly deny the historicity, asserting that all these are things that come to pass in all men's experience. Such indeed, are "the *erōtika* (Skr. śr̥ṅgāra into which, it seems that you, O Socrates, should be initiated," as Diotima says, and which in fact he so deeply respected.[34]

But this is not only a matter of Grace; the soul's salvation depends also on her submission, her willing surrender; it is prevented for so long as she resists. It is her pride (māna, abhimāna, οἴημα, οἴησις; "self-opinion, overweening"), the Satanic conviction of her own independence (asmi-māna, ahaṁkāra, cogito ergo sum), her evil rather than herself, that must be killed; this pride she calls her "self-respect," and would "rather die" than be divested of it. But the death that she at last, despite herself, desires, is no destruction but a transformation. Marriage is an initiatory death and integration (nirvāna, saṁskāra, τέλος).[35] "Der Drache und die Jungfrau sind natürlich identisch" [36]; the "Fier Baiser" transforms the dragon; the mermaid loses her ophidian tail; the girl is no more when the woman has been "made"; from the nymph the winged soul emerges.[37] And so, "through Thee an Iblis may become again one of the Cherubim." [38]

And what follows when the lower and higher forms of the soul have been united? This has nowhere been better described than in the *Aitareya Āraṇyaka* (2.2.7): "This Self gives itself to that self, and that self to this Self; they become one another; with the one form he (in whom this marriage has been consummated) is unified with yonder world, and with the other united to this world"; the Br̥hadāraṇyaka Upanishad (4.3.23): "Embraced by the Prescient-Self, he knows neither a within nor a without. Verily, that is his form in which his desire is obtained, in which the Self is his desire, and in which no more desires or grieves." "Amor ipse non quiescit, nisi in amato, quod fit, cum obtinet ipsum possessione plenaria," [39] "Jam perfectam animam . . . gloriosam sibi sponsam Pater conglutinat." [40] Indeed:

Dafern der Teufel könnt aus seiner Seinheit gehn,
So sähest du ihn stracks in Gottes Throne stehn.[41]

Inasmuch as the Devil is able to go out of his Being,
Thou wouldst immediately see him standing before the throne of God.
(Trans. by Ed.)

So, then, the Agathos and Kakos Daimons, Fair and Foul selves, Christ and Antichrist, both inhabit us, and their opposition is within us. Heaven and Hell are the divided images of Love and Wrath *in divinis*, where the Light and the Darkness are undivided, and the Lamb and the Lion lie down together. In the beginning, as all traditions testify, heaven and earth were one and together; essence and nature are one in God, and it remains for every man to put them together again within himself.

All these are our answers. Satan is not a real and single Person, but a severally postulated personality, a "Legion." Each of these personalities is capable of redemption (apokatastasis), and can, if it will, become again what it was before it "fell"—Lucifer, Phosphorus, Hēlēl, Scintilla, the Morning Star, a Ray of the Supernal Sun —because the Spark, however it may seem to be smothered, is an Asbestos that cannot be extinguished, even in hell. But in the sense that a redemption of all beings cannot be thought of as taking place at any one time, and inasmuch as there will be devilish souls in need of redemption throughout all time, Satan must be thought of as being damned forever, meaning by "damned," self-excluded from the vision of God and the knowledge of Truth.

The problem with which we started has been largely solved, but it still remains to accomplish the harder tasks of an actual "self-naughting" and consequent "Self-realization" to which the answers point, and for which theology is only a partial preparation. Satan and the Ego are not really entities, but concepts postulated and valid only for present, provisional, and practical purposes; both are composite photographs, as it were of X_1, X_2, X_3. It has often been said that the Devil's most ingenious device is to persuade us that his existence is a mere "superstition." In fact, however, nothing can be more dangerous than to deny his existence, which is real, although no more so than our own; we dare not deny Satan until we have denied ourselves, as everyone must who would follow Him who said and did "nothing of himself." "What is Love? the sea of nonexistence" [42]; and "whoever enters there, saying 'It is I,' I (God) smite him in the face" [43]; "What is Love? thou shalt know when *thou* becomest *Me*." [44]

NOTES

1. Margaret Marshall, in *The Nation*, February 2, 1946.
2. Jacob Boehme, *De incarnatione Verbi*, 2.5.18.

3. *Idem.*, *Dialogues*, "The Supersensual Life," and "Of Heaven and Hell," and "A Discourse . . ." Everyman's Library Edition, especially pages 259, 260, but all should be read.

4. "Person cannot be affirmed . . . of living things . . . bereft of intellect and reason . . . but we say there is a person of a man, of God, of an Angel" (Boethius, *Contra Eutychen*, 2). On this basis, Satan, who remains an Angel even in Hell, can be called a Person, or indeed, Persons, since his name is "Legion: for we are many"; but as a fallen being, "out of his right mind," in reality a Person only potentially. Much the same could be said of the soul, viz., that there is a Person of the soul, but hardly that the soul, as it is in itself, is a Person. Satan and the soul, both alike invisible, are only "known," or rather "inferred," from behavior, which is just what "personality" implies: "personality, that is the hypothetical unity that one postulates to account for the doings of people" (H. S. Sullivan, "Introduction to the Study of Interpersonal Relations," *Psychiatry*, 1, 1938).

5. Plato, *Republic* 439 D, E, 604 B; Philo, *Det.* 2; St. Thomas Aquinas, *Summa Theol.* II, 26.4; St. Paul, II Cor. 4:16; and in general, as the doctrine is briefly stated by Goethe: "Zwei Seelen wohnen ach, in meiner Brust, die eine will sich von der andern trennen" (Faust, I, 759). Similarly in the Vedanta, Buddhism, Islam, and in China.

6. *Nil agit in seipsum*: axiomatic in Platonic, Christian and Indian philosophy: "the same thing can never do or suffer opposites in the same respect or in relation to the same thing at the same time," Plato, *Republic*, 436 B; "strictly speaking, no one imposes a law upon his own actions," St. Thomas Aquinas, *Sum. Theol.* 1.93.5; "because of the antinomy involved in the notion of acting upon oneself" (svātmani ca kriyāvirodhāt), Sankara on BG 2.17.

7. "Art thou free of self? then art thou 'Self-governed'" (*selbes gewaltic =* Skr. svarāṭ), Meister Eckhart (Pfeiffer), p. 598.

8. "How can that which is never in the same state 'be' anything?" (Plato, *Cratylus*, 439 E: *Theatetus*, 152 D; *Symposium*, 207 D, etc.) "Ego" has no real meaning, because it is perceived only for an instant," *i.e.*, does not last for even so long as two consecutive moments (naivāham-arthaḥ kṣanikatva-darsanāt, Vivekacūḍāmani, 293).

9. It is unfortunate that, in modern psychology, an originally lucid terminology and distinction has been confused by an equation of the "soul-image" with "the *anima* in man, the *animus* in woman." The terms are even more misused by Father D'Arcy in his *Mind and Heart of Love*, ch. 7. Traditionally, *anima* and *animus* are the "soul" and the "spirit" equally in any man or any woman; so William of Thierry (*cf.* note 22 below) speaks of *animus vel spiritus*. This usage goes back to Cicero, *e.g.* Tusc. I. 22. 52, Neque nos corpora sumus. Cum igitur *nosce te* dicit, hoc dicit, *nosce animum tuum*, and V. 13.38, humanus animus decerptus est ex mente divina; and Accidius (*trag.* 296), sapimus animo, fruimur anima' sine animo, anima est debilis.

10. In all traditions, not excepting the Buddhist, this man and this woman are both equally capable of "fighting the good fight."

11. *Cf.* D. B. MacDonald, *Hebrew Philosophical Genius* (p. 139), "the lower, physical nature, the appetites, the psyche of St. Paul . . . 'self,' but always with that lower meaning behind it"; Grimm, *Greek-English Lexikon*

of the New Testament, s.v. ψυχικός ("governed by the sensuous nature subject to appetite and passion"); "anima . . . cujus vel pulchritudo vitrus, vel deformitas vitum est . . . mutabilis est" (St. Augustine, *De gen. ad litt.* 7.6.9. and *Ep.* 166.2.3.).

On the other hand, the "Soul" or "Self" as printed with the capital is Jung's "Self . . . around which it [the Ego] revolves, very much as the earth rotates around the sun . . . [its] superordinated subject" (*Two Essays on Analytical Psychology*, p. 268); not *a* being, but the inconnumerable and indefinable "Being of all beings."

We are never told that the mutable soul is immortal in the same timeless way that God is immortal, but only that it is immortal "in a certain way of its own" (secundum quemdam modum suum, St. Augustine, *Ep.* 166.2.3.). If we ask, Quomodo?, seeing that the soul is in time, the answer must be, "in one way only, viz., by continuing to become; since thus it can always leave behind it a new and other nature to take the place of the old" (Plato, *Symposium*, 207 D). It is only God, who is the Soul of the soul, that we can speak of as immortal absolutely (I Tim. 6:16). It is incorrect to call the soul "immortal" indiscriminately, just as it is incorrect to call any man a Genius; man has an immortal Soul, as he has a Genius, but the soul can only be immortalized by returning to its source, that is to say, by dying to itself and living to its Self; just as a man becomes a Genius only when he is no longer "himself."

12. Even the Hebrew Sāṭān ("opponent") is not a personal name.

13. *Contest of Homer and Hesiod*, 320, where the expression εὔνουν εἶναι σεαυτῷ = μετανοεῖν ("repentance," *i.e.*, "coming to be in one's right mind"), the opposite of παρανοεῖν.

14. The Self we mean when we tell a man who is misbehaving to "Be yourself" (ἐν σαυτῷ γενοῦ, Sophocles, *Philoctetes* 950), for "all is intolerable when any man forsakes his proper Self, to do what fits him not" (*Ibid.*, 902, 903).

15. C. G. Jung, *The Integration of Personality*, p. 274.

16. E. E. Hadley, in *Psychiatry*, 5 (1942), 133; citing also H. S. Sullivan, *op. cit.*, pp. 121–134: "emphasized individuality of each of us, 'myself.' Here we have the very mother of illusions, the ever-pregnant source of preconceptions that invalidate almost all our efforts to understand other people."

17. William Law, *The Spirit of Love*, and *An Address to the Clergy*, cited in Stephen Hobhouse, *William Law*, pp. 156, 219, 220.

18. Angelus Silesius, *Der Cherubinische Wandersmann*, 5.238.

19. E. D. Andrews, *The Gift to Be Simple*, p. 18; *cf.* p. 79, "That great big I, I'll mortify."

20. Boehme, *De inc. Verbi*, 1.12.20.

21. Plato, *Republic*, 588 C ff., where the whole soul is compared to such a composite animal as the Chimaera, Scylla, or Cerberus. In some respects the Sphinx might have been an even better comparison. In any case, the human, leonine, and ophidian parts of these creatures correspond to the three parts of the soul, in which "the human in us, or rather our divine part" should prevail; of which Hercules leading Cerberus would be a good illustration.

22. William of Thierry, *Epistle to the Brethren of Mont Dieu*, 50, 51.

23. *Kashf al-Mahjūb*, trans. R. A. Nicholson (Gibb Memorial Series, No.

XVII), p. 199; *cf.* p. 9, "the greatest of all veils between God and man."

24. For Abū Sā'īd, see R. A. Nicholson, *Studies in Islamic Mysticism,* p. 53.

25. R. A. Nicholson, *The Mathnawī of Jalālu'd Dīn Rūmī* (Gibb Memorial Series) 4.2, 4.4, 4.6, and *do.,* Text, 4.1, 4.3, 4.5. Citations are from Rumi 1.2617, 2.2525, 3.374, 2738, 3193, 4053 (nafs va saitān har dū ek īn būd'and); *cf.* 2.2272 f., 5.2919, 2939. The fundamental kinship of Satan and the Ego is apparent in their common claim to independent being; and "association" (of others with the God who only *is*) amounts, from the Islamic point of view, to polytheism (*ibid.,* 4.2675–7).

26. On the meaning of the "Synteresis," etymologically an equivalent of Skr. sam-tāraka, "one who helps to cross over," see, O. Renz, *Die Synteresis nach dem Hl. Thomas von Aquin* (Münster i.W., 1911).

27. Romans 7:14–23; James 4:7.

28. Saint Bonaventura, *Dominica prima post octavum epiphaniae,* 2.2. For the whole theme, see also my "On the Loathly Bride," Speculum, 20 (1945), pp. 391–404.

29. Pfeiffer, p. 288.

30. *Rig Veda,* 10.24.5.

31. *Satapatha Brāhmaṇa,* 10.5.2.12.

32. *Kaṭha Up.* 2.18.

33. Plotinus, *Enneads* 6.9.9.

34. Plato, *Symposium* 210A.

35. *Nirvāna, Jātaka* 1.60; *samskāra,* Manu 2.67; *telos,* Liddell and Scott, *s.v.,* VI. 2.

36. E. Siecke, *Drachenkämpfe,* p. 14.

37. For the Fier Baiser see the references in my "On the Loathly Bride," (*loc. cit.*). For the marriage, Meister Eckhart (Pfeiffer, p. 407) and Omikron, *Letters from Paulos* (New York, 1920), *passim.*

38. Rūmī, *op. cit.,* 4.3496.

39. Jean de Castel, *De adhaerendo Deo,* c. 12.

40. Saint Bernard, *De grad. humilitatis,* 7.21.

41. Angelus Silesius, *op. cit.,* 1.143. *Cf. Theologia Germanica,* ch. xvi: "If the evil Spirit himself could come into true obedience, he would become an angel [of light] again, and all his sin and wickedness would be blotted out."

42. Rūmī, *op. cit.,* 3.4723.

43. Shams-i-Tabrīz, Ode 28 in R. A. Nicholson, *Dīwāni Shamsi Tabrīz,* p. 115. "None has knowledge of each who enters that he is So-and-So," *Ibid.,* p. 61.

44. Rūmī, *op. cit.,* 2, Introduction.

Radu R. Florescu

THE DEVIL IN ROMANIAN LITERATURE AND FOLKLORE

THE ATTITUDE OF the Romanian people toward the problem of evil in general, and the devil in particular, has not preoccupied the minds of scholars. The reason for this omission in present-day Marxist society is obvious enough: the subject of the devil, as that of God, is simply taboo in a philosophy that has no place for the spiritual. Past neglect of this subject, however, has more complex answers. It is related to the psyche, the national character of the Romanian people, their untheological and unmetaphysical approach to life and death, and also perhaps to a national pride which has no room for evil, on the territory bound by the Danube River, Black Sea and Carpathian Mountains.

Following the heavy Dracula publicity resulting from the publication in 1972 of *In Search of Dracula*, nothing has offended the Romanians more than the frequent allusions to Transylvania as "vampire country" with the implied extension of that sobriquet to Romania itself.

VARIETIES OF ROMANIAN DEVILS

This study is limited to the treatment of the devil theme and the problem of evil in the thinking of the Romanian people and the more sophisticated interpretations expressed by the literati in a native literature which began in earnest only in the 19th century.

Though simplified in this way, it is still a complex problem and the subject has rarely been treated scientifically. Even a layman will be able to distinguish between the attitudes of the God-fearing peasants toward the misshapen medieval devil so often carved in wood and stone and the lighthearted, almost cynical, reaction of

69

the *illuminati* to that same devil following the 18th-century attacks by the *philosophes*. One should never make the mistake of assuming that Romania has been cut off at any time in its history from the many intellectual and religious currents of the West, whether it be the Renaissance, Reformation or the Enlightenment. Such currents, however, affected only the Establishment and not the masses comprising 90 per cent of the population. These rural peasants nonetheless contributed to the creation of a native mythology, with their community living in the Danubian plain and Transylvanian plateau since Dacian times. Their modes of thought were shaped by the territory in which they lived, by their ethnic pedigree, their language, their cultural, historic and religious inheritance. For instance, it would be fascinating to inquire as to the extent that current folk beliefs were influenced by the monotheistic cult of Zalmoxis and other Dacian deities.[1] Such beliefs grafted themselves onto the none too solid fabric of the disorganized Christianity of the second century when Dacia finally became part of the Roman Empire. The accidents of history have further deepened the furrows of exclusivity in national thought. What emerges is a collective wisdom, entirely *sui generis* in spite of its indebtedness to its neighbors, claiming to be closer to ultimate reality than Greek philosophy and unwilling to accept unquestioningly the cultural legacy of the West. In this sense, Romanian mythology—one of the richest and least understood in Europe—must be looked upon as an expression of the wisdom of the peasant masses.[2] Handed down from one generation to another by word of mouth since the formation of a Romanian language, these sagas of the peasants—expressed in terms of historical legends, pastoral tales or simple incantations against the forces of evil—profoundly stamped themselves upon the native Orthodox clergy. Being largely uneducated, the village priests' religious beliefs were molded by the *Weltanschauung* of the rural masses, a fact which gives Romanian Orthodoxy a mystical flavor all its own and distinguishes it from other Eastern churches.[3] In that sense, Romanianism and Orthodoxy can legitimately be linked in an intimate union.

I

As in other mythologies, one of the chief themes of native folklore is the struggle between the forces of good and evil, between God and Satan and their respective associates. This fundamental struggle is brought down to very terrestrial levels, much of it being fought on this earth in the householder's backyard. When so cast in human shape, the struggle for the winning of souls is the more dangerous, as the forces of Satan stand in battle array all around. For the good man, the devil's cohorts are at time so overbearing that compromise forms the only alternative. One should of course at all times be on the side of God, but one ought not for security's sake to completely alienate the devil. A popular Romanian proverb states: "God is great, but you must not offend the devil."

What, then, is the peasant's conception of the devil and the devil's associates? There are, of course, various kinds of devils and a great number of spirits of evil inseparable from the devil himself.

The Bogomil devil, co-creator of the universe, is somewhat implied in peasant reverential attitudes: one may, in fact, light a small candle to him since *he* is powerful too. The Biblical devil, God's fallen angel Lucifer, is represented simply to satisfy the quest for an historical explanation of how the devil was chased into the bowels of the earth where his headquarters lay. Always present is the devil as tempter on the left side of man, waging daily battle with the guardian angel and ready to resort to Pucklike tricks to cheat the good angel. The associates of the devil are most to be feared, since they lurk everywhere and exercise their evil force more directly upon man.

The devil and his accomplices are known by a greater variety of names than in almost any other language.[4] Some of the terms are borrowed from abroad. In the three provinces that comprise modern Romania (Transylvania, Moldavia and Wallachia) one can count seventy-two different names. The most frequently used is, of course, *Dracul* (from the Greek "Dragon"), with a Latin *Diavol* considered more literary. There follows *Belzebut*, *Satane*, both international in character. A generic term frequently used for the devil is *Necuratul* meaning "the unclean one." (The word *Nosferatul* which Bram Stoker had contemplated as the original title for his novel *Dracula*, published in 1897, may be a corruption of that word.) The devil is often identified with Romania's enemies; such is the word *Tartar* frequently used by the peasants. There are words supposedly descriptive of his physiognomy, such as *Cornut*, *Cel cu Coarne* ("the horned one") and *Codilă, Cel cu Coadă* ("the tailed one"). The more timorous allow for a moment's silence instead, afraid to mention his name. Others refer to him by mentioning the weapons used against the devil. Such is *Ucigăl*

Crucea meaning "the one meant to be killed by the cross," or
Ugigǎl Toaca, meaning "the one man meant to be killed by the
toacǎ," which is a wooden stick used tomtom fashion in the Orthodox monasteries to call the faithful to prayer.

The king of devils is not alone in tormenting the faithful. In hell
he has his legions, the angels of darkness; on earth he also controls
powerful associates; in fact, a specific vocabulary has been coined
for the devil's associates, almost as rich as the names used for the
devil himself. For the sake of convenience, we can divide the allies
of Satan into the following categories: [5]

1. The "little devils," the *Drǎcuşori* and *Spiriduşi,* are not very
clearly differentiated from Satan himself except in terms of powers
(each has his female equivalent. *Drǎcuşoarǎ, Diavoloaicǎ, Spiri-
duşǎ,* etc.).

2. The "black witches" come next: *Widme, Strigǎ, Vrǎjitoarǎ*
(even the more mythologized figure of *Muma Pǎdurii,* "the Mother
of the Forest," is in league with the devil).

3. The vampires and their female associates are creatures of the
night which cannot be separated from the demonic force.[6] The
classical "undead" or "reanimated corpse" type of vampire is the
Strigoi, a very ancient Romanian word derived from "witch." Even
the word for vampire, *Oupir* (of Serbian origin) is probably derived from the Turkish word for witch, *utter.* The *Strigoi* is condemned to survive on the blood of the living at night for varying
periods of time and remains in his coffin during the day. Although
Dom Augustin Calmet in his famous treatise on vampirism (Paris,
1751) speculated on whether vampires were the creatures of God
or the devil, the Romanian Orthodox Church believes that this is
in essence a folk superstition—the peasants' way of looking at a
punishment from God for various misdemeanors.[7]

In contrast to the undead vampire, *Strigoi,* there are the living
vampires, the *Moroi,* who have sold themselves to Satan by a formal compact, like the black witch, or have been doomed to vampirism since birth. Such creatures can leave their bodies at night
and consort with the undead vampires, witches and other devils.
They can be distinguished by their misshapen bodies, their red
hair, and eyebrows which meet over their nose.

4. The mythological vampires: the *Zmei,* the *Zburǎtor,* the
Vîrcolac and their various female equivalents such as the *Iele,* all
share some of the attributes of the devil and each does his "thing"
with powers extraterrestrial.[8] The *Vîrcolac* is a huge serpent which

reminds one of the Dragon God of the Dacians and can cause
eclipses of the sun and moon. The *Iele* are wicked fairies who play
during the night, cause disease and fade the very grass on which
they dance. The *Zburător* endowed with wings attacks beautiful
maidens at night like our movie vampire, leaving them dizzy and
faint when they wake up. All these unclean spirits make plans in
common when they meet for their *sabat*, particularly on certain
dangerous nights such as the Eve of St. Andrews (November 30)
when neither man nor beast is safe from their attack.

Despite such instances of devil fear, the unclean one is by no
means a figure of terror in Romanian folklore. After the failure of
his revolt in heaven, where he had, after all, been a favorite angel
of God, the devil was chased deep into earth where hell is located.
Like other spirits of evil, he is a creature of darkness and when
he surfaces he takes refuge within the bark of trees or at the bottom of stagnant waters—a frequent, indirect allusion to the devil
is "*Cel din Baltă*," meaning "the one who resides in the swamp."
Like his associates the vampires, he likes abandoned churches, the
tops of mountains and ruined castles. During the night when the
devil does most of his mischief, he meets with other spirits of evil
on the confines of villages and at crossroads, planning his program
after the clock strikes midnight and until the cock—a holy animal
in peasant mythology—crows for the third time, when presumably
all wicked spirits return into the earth.

In the crude peasant engravings, sculptures, or masks, the devil
looks evil but earthy. The color of his skin is black, he has horns, a
long tail, goat's legs and hoofs. Traditionally he is thin and ugly.
On occasion the devil can transform himself into a number of animals created by him, such as the wolf, the bat, the owl, the ram,
and especially the black cat. The animal world, as well as insects
and plants, is divided between the "holy" and the "unholy," unclean and useless. If the swallow, the deer, the pigeon, the cock,
the bee and most of the beautiful flowers have been created by
God, the black moths, the flies and all weeds are made by the devil
and will collaborate with him to create as much mischief as possible among men and beasts.

II

The devil, however, has his limitations in the fight that he daily
wages against God and the angels. Although clever, he is not

omniscient and he can occasionally be outwitted by men and women, particularly old women, whom he fears. In the devil's view, women are more "devilish" than men and "old hags more devilish than the devil," causing even him gray hairs. The word "dracul" is often used in popular interjections in a lighthearted matter-of-fact manner. A careful analysis of popular expressions and proverbs invoking the devil's name indicates daily acceptance of his presence.[9] Nor is he wholly black, and at times one almost feels compassion for him.

Of course in the struggle with God for the winning of souls, the devil has to play tricks and so he daily whispers in the peasant's left ear. He cheats lovers and spoils marriages; tempts the greedy by sprouting flames over buried treasures—the color of the flame varies with the nature of the precious metal or stone—on the Night of St. Andrew when vampires also play.[10] There are more wicked temptations: the devil can ensnare a priest with sex and alcohol. Finally, he can succeed by making a compact with a man or woman and surely will lead the individual astray, starting with venial temptations and ending up with crime. Should he fail he will of course take revenge; he can cause sickness, epilepsy, etc.[11] If he succeeds totally we would call it "possession," though the Romanian peasants avoid that word. The devil then guarantees certain advantages, the prolongation of life or material success, even though hell is the inevitable punishment. Like the vampire the devil also has the power of sex, consorting with witches and promising them a long lease on life. If he has children they are inevitably ugly, deformed and condemned to hell. In many areas of Romania the people believe that any monster or deformed child has the devil as his father and such children are therefore shunned.[12] If the devil is finally driven out of man, smoke will emerge from the victim's ears or mouth.

The peasant's conception of hell is in line with this terrestrial attitude toward spirits, whether good or evil, and most of the rewards as well as the sufferings are described in terms of physical enjoyment or intensive pain. Anyone wishing to visualize popular belief in a hedonistic paradise and a fiery hell should glance at the primitive ikons, murals and other forms of religious art within the humble village church and the remarkable 15th-century frescoes painted on the outer walls of monasteries, some of which have survived the cold winters of five centuries virtually unscathed.[13]

Surrounded as he is with evil, what talismans or forces can the peasant muster to cope with Satan and his cohorts? Traditionally there is, of course, the power of the Romanian Orthodox Church. However, unlike such Catholic countries as Spain and Ireland where the clergy has assumed an overwhelming spiritual, cultural and even political role, the *popa* is not always viewed with a kindly eye by the peasant. Part of the reason for that low esteem may be the uneducated state of the average country priest, who knows little beyond the Sunday liturgy. The village *curé* is in fact often a figure of fun for "the priest eats on living as well as dead" and occasionally he even brings bad luck, consequently you must avoid him.[14] The *popa* will pronounce curses, anathemas, and excommunications on people and objects, but in the village there is no formal ritual of exorcism.

Beyond the ritual, in which the church is deeply immersed, there is the power of the cross and the religious image or ikon. It would indeed be difficult to find in current Western theological literature a learned treatise entitled: *The Power of the Cross* or the *Intercession of Ikons*, a frequent theme in the pages of the official review of the Romanian Orthodox Church (*Biserica Ortodoxă Română*).[15] Bram Stoker's use of the symbolism of the cross in combatting vampires (immortalized on the screen in the 1931 Bela Lugosi movie) is borrowed straight from Romanian popular folklore. To this day in certain Transylvania villages peasants cross themselves three times over when they think they have seen *Necuratul* in any of his forms. Crosses are seen almost everywhere, beautifully carved in wood or engraved in metal. Single crosses and double or treble crosses called *troiţe* are to be found in courtyards, at fountains, crossroads, and pasture fields in the middle of nowhere to protect the sheep and cattle against evil spirits; also on porticos, doors, and thresholds of houses. Similar in nature is the power of ikons, particularly those depicting certain saints such as St. George, St. Haralambie, St. Toader, and particularly St. Elias, who chases devils out of the sky, cracking his whip in his smoke-ridden cart and thus causing thunder and lightning on his feast day (July 20).[16] The ikon or cross is more than just a memento of Romanian peasant piety, representing, rather, a mystical symbol enabling man to meet and call upon God for daily help.

Rather than relying solely on the priest, the people prefer to have their own experts in combatting the forces of evil, proven effective since pre-Christian times. The real experts in casting out devils are the old village women, the "white witches" in the New

England sense, not to be confused with the devil's associates.
Among the oldest weapons are the *descîntece*, a difficult word to
translate meaning "magic charm" or "exorcism." There are no less
than ninety *descîntece* in G. Dem Teodorescu's remarkable compi-
lation on Romanian folklore aimed at all kinds of *deochiu* or be-
witchment by the evil eye,[17] some of which can be traced back to
pagan Dacian practices. Incantations accompanied by a certain
rite, even the use of spittle and the boiling or application of herbs,
lovage, camomile, mandrake (there is a whole cult dedicated to
this specific plant [18]), and inevitably garlic (by far the most potent)
are frequently resorted to. "*Nuip cusnuip*," says the devil. "I will not
enter the house where garlic is consumed." "Beware of the man or
woman," states another proverb, "who habitually does not take
garlic, he may indeed be a living vampire." [19] It is interesting to
notice that medical practice has recently shown an increasing interest in the power of herbs to cure a great variety of physical ail-
ments—a simple confirmation of the collective wisdom of rural
medicine, which has known for years, for instance, that garlic
lowers blood pressure and activates the circulation of the blood.[20]
Saintly animals are also sacrificed, such as the cock whose morning crow chases the devil away. The cock may be killed on the site
of a suspected vampire's tomb. Other antidotes against wicked
spirits are light (since evil spirits belong to the dark), which is one
reason why torches are kept ablaze on the Night of St. Andrew;
noise, as the ringing of church bells, and the beating of tomtoms of
the *toacă*. All this frightens the devil away. The ultimate weapon
against vampires is of course the stake through the heart, the
method used by St. George in destroying the devil—and by Dracula
in killing his political enemies. Stakes are presumed to rivet evil
spirits solidly to the ground, thus preventing their nightly pursuits
by finally liberating their souls. In a few cemeteries one can still
find decorated wooden stakes encircling a suspect's grave to bottle
up the snake holes through which vampires may emerge at night.

III

Handed down from one generation to another by word of mouth,
like the Scandinavian sagas, this extraordinarily rich Romanian
folk mythology deserves to be highlighted, since it reflects the soul
of the people. In addition, and in default of a written language and
literature, folklore fills a void and provides an obvious source of

inspiration. The formal religious literature in Slavonic and later in Greek has little or no contact with the peasantry, nor for that matter has the foreign-educated Establishment, borrowing its ideas from the West. Perhaps the earliest contact between the people on the one hand and princes and boyars on the other was effected by the Romanian equivalent of the Western troubadours and meistersingers who presented their allegorical plays, dances and nativity scenarios with dance and mask at court. Drawn from popular themes the devils and the good angels both had an important role in the development of these folk-act norms.[21]

Romania owes its first books in the written language to the efforts of the 16th-century Lutheran Reformation when a catechism was translated into the vernacular.[22] Luther's obsession with the problem of the devil and his anti-ritualist theology failed to awaken much of a response because it was not in tune with peasant philosophy. The villager knew the devil too intimately to be terrorized! Peasant fetishisms were too deeply ingrained to look at faith as the only solution to the problem of evil. This is obviously too simplistic an answer to the complex problem as to why the Protestant Reformation failed to gain over the Romanians of Transylvania, for it did succeed in converting a good many Hungarians and Germans. The Catholic Church was somewhat more successful in its inroads, and a large segment of Romanian Orthodox clergy accepted a union with Rome in 1699, on condition of preserving their ritual and their language.[23] Among the fringe benefits of that union, from the Romanian point of view, lay the possibility of a few sons of priests going to Rome for their theological studies at the College of *Propagande Fide* and elsewhere. Within this group of young theologians was Ion Budai-Deleanu, a kind of Chaucer of the Romanian language at that time in literary formation, and the author of the first heroic-comic-epic written in the native tongue, entitled *Tiganiada*, completed at the close of the 18th century but published years later. By a weird coincidence, Dracula, the devils, vampires, and even a member of the author's family, a Florescu, have roles in this work.[24] These roles, however, are not at all those expected by the movie-indoctrinated 20th-century American audience. Dracula and his army of gypsies, together with Florescu, are on the side of the angels, while their antagonists are the devils, vampires and Turks (the devil is referred to as *Satana*, and the *Strigoi* and the female species make their debut in Romanian literature). Although Budai-Deleanu was a convert to Catholic theology, the influences of his

myth-centered Transylvanian background with its eerie spirits, its
sinister castle and moon-shaped mountains of the Retezat, form
the poetic substratum to the newly found theology of the Jesuits
and the political thinking of the Enlightenment. Foreign influences
are to be found in the poem, nevertheless, in some of the Voltairean
irony toward the devil. The gypsy hero, Parpangel, has, at least,
free commuting powers to travel from heaven to hell.

The new current of Transylvanian Latinism which created a
written Romanian language found its way to the other two provinces, Moldavia and Wallachia—still slumbering in oriental leth-
argy—by way of some of these Transylvanian educators, who were
the true creators of a Romanian national consciousness. In the two
older provinces, they were competing with several other currents of
thought: among these, the traditional ecclesiastical culture, both
Slavonic and Greek, devoid of any national roots, and the upper-
class intelligentsia, largely the product of the French Enlightenment.

Under the impact of their partially digested sophistication, the
upper class looked down upon peasant "primitivism" and was condescending in its attitude to "village philosophy." The Transyl-
vanians, who centered their nationalism upon native roots, were in
turn full of irony toward these "bonjourists" as they qualified them.
Within the circle of the sophisticated few, we can of course find
facile imitations and translations of all aspects of Western, and
particularly French, treatment of the devil theme: the lame devil of
the illuminati, the Romantic devil of de Vigny, the Mephistophelian
devil, and even occultism of the type that has recently assailed the
United States. These are, however, insignificant trends, birds singing foreign songs with little or no impact in the land, in contrast to
"la grande littérature."

Romanian literature was born in the 19th century, deriving its
inspiration almost entirely from folkloric themes. All the evil
forces enumerated above are present, though at a more sophisticated level with more precise words and within the context of a
more refined language. Satan and his cohorts figure under a wide
variety of titles and themes from the 19th century to our time.
Hardly a poet, novelist or playwrite of note has successfully
evaded the subject of the devil. A long list of names will be meaningful only to the Romanian reader. The poets D. Bolintineanu
and B. Delavrancea dealt extensively with Satan himself; others
like I. Eliade-Rădulescu, I. Văcărescu, C. Petrescu, V. Eftimiu, Al.

Brătescu-Voinești and A. Maniu preferred the mythological aspects of the *Necuratul* centering their prose and poetry on the *Iele* (evil fairies), the *Sburător* (winged vampire), the *Vîrcolac*, the *Zmeu* (dragon-type monster) or the simple *Piaza Rea*, the spirit of sheer bad luck which obsessed Caragiale.[25] Others yet, like Sorbul, found roles for demons or demon-like creatures on the stage, while Tudor Arghezi concentrated on the curses of peasants against all evil forces.

IV

One may attempt to highlight the literary approach to popular mythology with a few specific instances. The leitmotif of the poem *Ielele* written by Iancu Văcărescu is the "satanic burlesque." These creatures are so infuriatingly wicked that, in the end, even some of the devils shout that the *Iele* be roasted alive.[26]

In one of Eliade-Rădulescu's *chef-d'oeuvre*, *Sburătorul*, the love-smitten mythological vampire is caught in the act of sexual aggression and the divine comedy ends with a massive revolt of the spirits of evil against the powers of good. Vasile Alexasandri's poems and ballads are largely inspired from folklore, full of mythological landscapes, satanic cavalcades, dragons and living dead. Alexandru Sihleanu, a minor poet compared to Alexsandri, centers a whole ballad on a sanguinary encounter between two vampire knights struggling all night for the possession of their victim in the ruins of a devil-possessed castle.

One of the most eloquent of the macabre exponents of all species of evil was assuredly the Romantic poet and revolutionary, Dimitrie Bolintineanu. In his case the spirits of the night emerged from their shadowy refuges in a kind of terrestrial inferno, also written in ballad form. The Carpathian *sabat* takes place in some mountain cave to the tune of the hooting owl. Then, the assembled forces of darkness made their plans, the devil and his cohorts dance on the mountaintop, roar at the moon, the stars and the clouds. Other mythological figures attend this infernal banquet, "with head of a bull, claws of vampire and tail of dragon." The devils are there by the legion, "six legions of them flying like in a whirlwind and laughing with a roar, oh, with what a roar! Quite an infernal orchestration." [27]

Not all the writers tackled evil in such sinister terms, and the natural good humor of the peasant reasserts itself at the village level in the works of Ion Creangă, a peasant from the mountain village of Humuleşti, and those of Barbu Delavrancea, a farmer from the neighborhood of Bucharest. The latter has a funlike story entitled, "Coada Dracului" or "The Tail of the Devil," reducing Satan once again to human proportions. A little baby devil was being breast fed by mother devil who cuddled him in her arms. The only embarrassment was baby devil's tail, excessively long, serpentine, and meandering along the valleys and mountains of Romania. The tip of the tail, which was invisible, stood in the middle of a dusty road at the edge of a certain village. A poor peasant with his cart overfilled with logs collided straight into the little devil's tail, broke the axle and wheels of his cart, and quite naturally started cursing, listing all the devil's names from Belzebut downwards. The little one looked his mother straight in the eye and said: "See here, Mother, how good I have been lying on your bosom, drinking your milk at the bottom of hell and all these humans swear at me!" "Yes," answered the devil mother. "It's true, my little one, that you were good and went to bed last night in my lap, but why did you leave your tail hanging outside?" [28] Following the same theme of the devil's humanity, which is persistent in Romanian folklore, two famous peasant rogues, Păcală and Ţăndală, constantly succeed in outwitting the evil one with their cunning.[29]

Leaving Satan himself under his various disguises, what of the literary treatment of the devil within the wider context of the "devil"—or "possessed"—personality of history. Having recently co-authored two books on a 15th-century ruler nicknamed "Dracula" which means "son of the devil," the topic naturally suggests itself. Bram Stoker, the 19th-century Anglo-Irish novelist, patterned his *Dracula* on an unscientific mixture of history and folklore, and implied on the basis of certain alleged documents that this Dracula was a vampire in league with "the evil one." [30] Research of the authentic Dracula archive revealed no such evidence of "possession." Dracula's father, Dracul ("the devil"), may have been given that cognomen for certain evil deeds unknown to history. However, a far more logical explanation of that sobriquet, inherited by the son, is the fact that in 1431 the father was invested with the Order of the Dragon with the objective of fighting Hussites and Moslems and the obligation of wearing the dragon standard on certain days.[31] The peasants, seeing the unfamiliar emblem, coined the epithet "Dracul" since the dragon was the symbol of Satan. Neither Dracul nor Dracula has really aroused literary interest along the lines of the "possession" theme. The closest we come to a Satanic hero is in the novel of Alexander Odobescu entitled Mihnea "the Bad," the name of Dracula's son. The play ends with the father agonizing amidst the rattling of the chains of his dying slaves.[32] There are, of course, better known historical devils who have become the center of literary plots. Such is the novel *Alexandru Lăpuşneanu* by C. Negruzzi, the story of a villainous prince doomed to spill blood indiscriminately. In the same category is *Prince Despot*, an incredibly diabolical Greek who inspired one famous drama by Vasile Alecsandri as he plans to capture the throne by foul play.

Two other literary genres connected with the devil affected Romanian literature, though only in a superficial manner and could well be dismissed as literary importations from abroad. They do, nevertheless, deserve a few words of comment. One is the Romanian equivalent of the Gothic horror theme increasingly in vogue in the West from the time of Walpole's *Castle of Otranto*, and of course extended in popular range in 1921 with the first silent movie based on Stoker's plot—F. Murnau's *Nosferatu*. Strange as it may seem, the demon *Nosferatu* or *Necuratul* and his bloodcurdling vampire associates, though placed on Transylvanian soil by the Anglo-Irish author who created them, never took solid anchor in the heart or imagination of the Romanian public; nor did the Gothic format succeed in inspiring significant works. Given the enormous popularity of Bram Stoker's novel in the West (it has never been out of print since it was first published in 1897), it is little short of ironic that as late as 1932 a Romanian scholar writing in the prestigious *Historical Journal* could speculate on the possibility that *Dracula*, the very famous motion picture starring Bela Lugosi in 1931, could have been inspired by a Hungarian scenario writer.[33] In spite of the fact that Bram Stoker's book had been translated virtually into every major European language, it took the stir created by *In Search of Dracula* in 1972 to get the Stoker novel translated into Romanian the following year.[34]

There is a vague Radcliffian debut in Romanian literature in the verse of the poet Grigore Alexandrescu who was obsessed with old castles and ruined abbeys where the devil was thought to habitually reside. The mythological vampire appears almost Gothic in his sinister eroticism in a poem entitled "Vampires" written by Mihail Eminescu, the greatest of Romanian writers, who died prematurely at the age of thirty-nine.[35] However, the closest Romanian approximation to Bram Stoker is Duliu Zamfirescu *par excellence* the exponent of the sinister forces which animate the demonic vampire that provides such a contrast to the almost chummy devil of popular folklore. Like Stoker, Zamfirescu admitted to being in a wicked frame of mind when writing—an experience shared by Bela Lugosi in his acting. (This may be the reason for the advice of the poet Cosbuc "not to research evil, for if you do you become insane!") Such titles as *The Vampires, The Castle of Death, The Bride of the Vampire* are representative of Zamfirescu's writings, but his works awakened no deep spark among his readers and were hardly best-sellers. It is interesting and rather significant to note in passing that the Romanian studios have yet to produce a film of the nature of the numerous *Draculas* or *The Exorcist* and that no English or American vampire import has lately been shown in Bucharest or Cluj.

By way of contrast a few comments on the treatment of the devil as a vehicle for satire are in order—this was yet another literary importation following Satan's dethronement in the West during the post-Romantic era (not to be confused with the peasant's "pulling the devil's leg" approach). One late 19th-century satirist, N. T. Orășanu, exploited this subject to the point of boredom, though with a certain diablerie which offended the authorities, who were usually the butts of his sarcasm. He began by giving his satirical periodical the devil's more conventional name. As each issue was suppressed, he would simply substitute one of the many other names of the evil one, *Nichipercea, Sarsailă, Codita*, etc., to elude pursuit and temporarily fool the authorities. Others tried to reduce the devil to minor proportions of fun. Such were the attempts of an ex-monk D. Stănoiu whose witticisms were aimed at holy men and priests tempted in the form of well-seasoned macaroni dishes with God's punishments confined to kidney stones.[36] Interestingly enough the droll devil was no more successful than the Radcliffian devil.

Very much the same thing is true of Satanist and occult practices and writings, even those dealing with the mysticism of the Far East, the drug culture and sex. They have simply failed to awaken a deep responsive chord in Romania, perhaps because the people have always experienced a unique mysticism all their own. For the peasant there are no final metaphysical or theological problems; he simply accepts God's fate, for he knows the world is ruled by forces man cannot control or understand.

It might be retorted, of course, that Satanism—even if popular —would officially be frowned upon by a Marxist materialist government. This leads to a few concluding thoughts concerning the use of the devil's name when Satan is identified as the enemy of the established regime, in the sense of the Kaiser or Hitler being literally painted in the image of the devil. Since the writing of history is a matter of dates, sometimes the devils of yesterday have a way of becoming the angels of tomorrow. Each generation, of course, sets the Satanic rules and writes about him in terms of the passions, or remaining residual passions, of his era. Caragiale, possibly Romania's greatest dramatist, in his play *Kir Ianulea* saw the devil in the nasty Greek Fanariot princes who exploited the country during the 18th century; whereas the pamphleteer Orășanu and the poet Eminescu saw him in the amoral politicians of the late 19th century (Eminescu calls Dracula back to life to impale them). The poet in exile, Ion Feraru, saw the sinister force in the fascist regime responsible for the death of countless Jews working on the infernal canal which attempted to link the Danube River to the Black Sea. To Virgil Gheorghiu in his *25th Hour* the devil is assuredly the blind bureaucratic machine, whether German or American, which reduces man to a number. Refugees from Stalinist persecution camps, such as Nimigeanu and R. S. Rubsel, wrote about the *Inferno on Earth* implied in the early years of the Communist regime.

If the present rulers of Romania were allowed to believe in the devil, they would see his hand in the decadence and lack of moral fiber of Western culture which they are determined to resist by insisting that culture and art seek inspiration only on native soil. The problem is, however, that they cannot invoke the devil, since he is not kosher in a Marxist society. But, then, how does one explain him away in a nation which has believed in him for a thousand years or more? You may indeed attempt to strike the forces of history with the devil's three-pronged pitchfork, but he has an uncanny way of hitting back.

NOTES

1. The pre-Christian cult of the Dragon Snake still survives in such peasant proverbs as: "Do not kill the garden snake, for it will bring you bad luck." A good treatment of Zalmoxis, the Dacian deity, is Mircea Eliade's *Zalmoxis, the Vanishing God* (Chicago: Univ. of Chicago Press, 1972).

2. For a good introduction to Romanian folklore, see G. Nandriș, "Romanian Folklore," *The Aryan Path* (April 1954), pp. 164–169.

84   RADU R. FLORESCU

3. There are few good studies on Romanian Orthodoxy: A convenient historical sketch by a leading Byzantinist is M. Beza, *The Romanian Church* (London, 1934). The author stresses the role of Orthodoxy in preserving national culture.

4. A rich collection of expressions concerning the devil can be found in *Dicţonar de expresii şi locuţiuni Româneşti,* (Bucharest, 1969) p. 130 and *Proverbe Româneşti,* (Bucharest, 1967) pp. 152–153.

5. Scientific literature on the devil is scanty in Romanian, almost non-existent in English. One, though inadequate, treatment is: A. Murgoci and H. Murgoci, "The Devil in Romanian Folklore," *Folklore,* Vol. 40, (1929). Also see Tudor Pamfile, *Diavolul Învrăjbitor al lumii* (Bucharest, 1914).

6. The vampire is adequately treated by A. Murgoci, "The Vampire in Romania," *Folklore,* Vol. 37, and G. Nandriş, "The Dracula Theme." For Bram Stoker's sources of inspiration, see Emily Gérard, *The Land Beyond the Forest,* London, 1888.

7. Dom Augustin Calmet, *Traité sur les apparitions des esprits et sur les vampires ou les revenants de Hongrie, de Moravie,* etc. (Paris, 1751), Vol. III, p .140.

8. Most of these terms are best defined in *Dicţionarul Limbii Române* (Bucharest, 1934), Vol. II, Part II F–I. For the word *Iele* and other terms not covered in the printed volume, see the same dictionary in manuscript at the Institute of Linguistics, Academy of the Romanian Socialist Republic.

9. M. Olănescu, *Mitologie românească* (Bucharest, 1944), p. 37. Other familiar expressions concerning the devil are:

"A băga cineva în draci" (to intimidate)

"Sunt plin de draci" (I am nervous)

"A da la toţi dracii (to manifest hostility)

"Al dracului" (beyond all measure or extremely capable)

"S'a dus dracului" (he left without leaving an address)

"Face şi pe dracul" (to be capable of)

"Dă-l dracului" (to give up)

"Parcă a întrat dracul în el or "A-i veni cuiva toţi dracii" (to get angry)
                              Dicţionar de expresii, p. 130.

10. Once a year on the Night of St. Andrew all treasures are supposed to burn (se joacă comorile)—the color of the flame being different for each kind of treasure (*i.e.,* a red flame for copper, ruby yellow for gold, and green for emerald). The treasures can only be dug up through the intercession of the cross and by sprinkling holy water to chase the devil away—otherwise finding them brings bad luck since the devil is in possession. The devil also lurks in abandoned castles and ruined abbeys, as does the vampire. Olănescu, *Mitologie româneasca,* p. 117. For buried treasures, see Nandriş, "The Dracula Theme in the European Literature of the West and East," *Literary History and Literary Criticism,* edited by L. Edel (New York, 1965).

11. Olănescu, *Mitologie românească*, p. 36.

12. "In Vîlcea, any monster that is born is supposed to have the devil as his father," Murgoci, "The Devil in Romanian Literature," p. 143.

13. The nature of the punishment imposed in hell fits the specific sin. Someone, for instance, who habitually lies has an adder dropping poison in his mouth. Popular ditties all describe very physical punishments: "I have seen my loved one" says one song, "with five devils beating and torturing her while red blood was running from her body." The external mural of Voroneţ Church (15th century) in Moldavia has a vivid portrayal of punishment in hell. For details of reproduction, see Maria A. Musicescu and S. Ulea, *Voroneţ* (Bucharest, 1969), p. 49.

14. *Proverbe românesti*, p. 322.

15. GH. Versescu, "Crucea în tradiţia poporului nostru" *Biserica Ortodoxă Română* (Oct. 1931), ser. II, XLIX, n. 10, 607, p. 595.

16. C. Irimie and M. Focsa, *Romanian Icons Painted on Glass* (Bucharest, 1969) pp. 128–130.

17. G. Dem. Teodorescu, *Poesii Populare Române Culegere* (Bucharest 1885), p. 355.

18. For the powers of mandrake, see M. Eliade, "The Cult Mandragora in Romania," *The University of Chicago Magazine* (Jan.-Feb., 1973), pp. 8–16.

19. Murgoci, "The Vampire in Romania," p. 321.

20. Many of the Romanian "descîntece" against physical and emotional disease use a great variety of herbs. Teodorescu, "Noţiuni despre descântece" in *Poezii*, p. 356 *et seq.*

21. *Istoria Literaturii Române* (Bucharest, 1964), p. 67.

22. G. Ivaşcu, *Istoria Literaturii Române* (Bucharest, 1968), p. 100.

23. Radu R. Florescu, "The Uniate Church, Catalyst of Romanian National Consciousness," *Slavonic and East European Review*, Vol. XLV, Nr 105 (July 1967), pp. 324–342.

24. song III—*"Florescul spune de ţigani s-alte*
        A lui *Vlad* tocmeli si fapte înalte"
    song IV—"Florescu mai spuné de a lui Vlad birunţe făcute
        Curtea măiastră prin o minune
        Piere ca *dracul* de *crucea sfîntă"*
    Ion Budai-Delenau, *Ţiganiada* (Bucharest, 1959), pp. 67 and 117.

25. There are many examples of the treatment of the devil, of mythological monsters and vampires in Romanian literature. The following are a few of the more famous titles: G. Azachi, *Turnul lui But*; Văcărescu, *Piaza Rea* and *Ielele*; I Eliade-Rădulescu, *Sburătorul*; D. Bolintineanu, *Mihnea şi baba*; C. Petrescu, *Sburătorul*; V. Eftimiu, *Inşirte-te Margarite*; Al. Brătescu-Voineşti, *Vîrcolacul*; I. Agîrbiceanu, *Strigoiul*; V. Demetrius, *Strigoiul*, etc.

26. G. Călinescu, *Istoria Literaturii Române* (Bucharest, 1968), p. 58.

27. D. Bolintineanu, *Scrieri alese*, ed. D. Popovici (Craiova, 1942).

28. B. Delavrancea, *Codiţa Dracului*.

29. J. Ure, *Pacala and Tandala and other Romanian Folktales* (London, 1960).

30. Bram Stoker, *Dracula* (New York, 1899).

31. R. T. McNally and R. Florescu, *In Search of Dracula* (Greenwich,

1972), pp. 22–23. R. Florescu and R. T. McNally, *Dracula, a Biography of Vlad the Impaler 1431–1476* (New York, 1973), pp. 30–31.

32. R. Florescu, "Dracula in Romanian Literature" to be published by the *East European Quarterly* in 1974.

33. F. Brînzau, "Vlad l'Empaleur dans litérature Turque," *Revista Istorică Română* (1946), XIV, p. 70.

34. Bram Stoker's *Dracula* was translated into Romanian by Dan Cioculescu.

35. Mihail Eminescu, *Opere Poezii* (Bucharest, 1933), p. 75.

36. G. Călinescu, *op. cit.*, p. 301.

Carter Lindberg

MASK OF GOD AND PRINCE OF LIES: LUTHER'S THEOLOGY OF THE DEMONIC

A STUDENT ONCE BEGAN an exam for me with these words of wisdom: "Be it ever so narrow, there is no place like history." *Mutatis mutandis*, one might ask what place an essay on Luther's theology of the demonic has in a collection of essays on the contemporary experience of the demonic. I can only assert at this point that few men in Western history have so profoundly expressed the dialectical, tension-filled nature of God and Satan, the holy and the demonic, good and evil, as did Luther. In his study, *The Idea of the Holy*, Rudolf Otto expressed his indebtedness to Luther,[1] and Paul Tillich claimed that Luther of all the Reformers most maintained the depth, mystery, and numinous character of the holy.[2] The litany of famous men could go on, but it will be sufficient to let Luther speak for himself. In the midst of the disruption, conflict, self-destruction, and despair of the sixteenth century (a milieu not unlike our own) Luther could say: "It is through living, indeed through dying and being damned that one becomes a theologian, not through understanding, reading or speculation."[3]

Thus *contra* the assumptions of my student and others, our interest in Luther's experiential theology of the demonic is by no means antiquarian. His experience is remarkably like the experience of many men today. While we cannot simply repristinate his conflict and its solution, we may nevertheless find clues in Luther to the meaning of our own experience. Some may balk at this, wondering how a man who threw inkpots at the devil may help us who have seen our brothers both walk on the moon and engage in genocide. First, some demythologizing is in order. The inkpot story ranks with that of the Dutch boy and the dike—neither really holds any water. While Luther certainly speaks frequently of the devil in his writings, no one has yet found a reference to this incident in Luther's own works. In fact, the famous inkpot proved to be such a great story that inkstains soon appeared in various Luther rooms for the benefit of tourists—and are frequently re-inked for the benefit of same! [4] Nevertheless, the story is not without merit, for it illustrates the modern temper to dismiss speech about evil which is not limited to moral or social-cultural categories. From the time of the Enlightenment to the present, Luther's theology of the demonic has been viewed in terms of his *Zeitgeist*, i.e., as a hangover of medieval superstition, or else as a case-study for whatever psychological or psychoanalytic axe a particular scholar wished to grind. Men of the Enlightenment could celebrate Luther as the founder of German nationalism and the defender of freedom of conscience. But to a people for whom religion ought to exist within the limits of reason alone, it was definitely a remnant of medieval mentality which spoke of evil and the demonic in theological and ontological terms. This was a wine which could burst their moral wineskins. For modern Roman Catholic detractors of Luther, the psychological and psychoanalytic explanation of why he broke with the Establishment was much more appealing and sophisticated than the crude diatribes of earlier Catholic apologists. So Luther has been interpreted as manic-depressive and psychotic; why else would someone exhibit such "sick" behavior as a revolt against the Establishment? [5] More recent are the well-known psychoanalyses of Luther by Erik Erikson [6] and Norman O. Brown.[7] The former uses a basically Freudian approach to analyze Luther's anxieties as a case of youthful identity crisis. Here, Luther's anxiety becomes a case study for the adolescent identity crisis and the working through of the problems of intimacy, generativity, and integrity. Luther's "solution" is the concept of a "gracious God" which replaces the stern father of his youth. A much more vivid analysis, and one which takes the reality of the demonic quite seriously, is the "metaphysically" Freudian account by Brown. Here, Luther is presented as an anal character whose idea of the devil is a mix of medieval superstition, personal experience, and theological speculation. Brown is convinced that psychoanalysis has not paid sufficient attention to the devil figure as an anal character. For Brown, Luther's recognition of this makes him the "most representative man of the age." "The Devil is virtually recognized as a materialization of Luther's own anality, which is to be conquered by being replaced where it came from." [8] Brown is by no means unsympathetic to Luther, and indeed bemoans contemporary Protestantism's loss of Luther's insight into anality, *i.e.*, his unmasking and repudiation of Western man's attempt at self-salvation through sublimation.

These attempts to explain (or explain away!) Luther's thought and work, fascinating and illuminating as they sometimes are, are ultimately inadequate. Luther's primary orientation is religious. Sociological, historical, psychological, and psychoanalytic interpretations may shed more or less light, but unless Luther's problem is recognized as a religious problem it will always be distorted, whatever one's hermeneutic may be. Luther lived and worked as a theologian, and wished to be understood and interpreted as a theologian. To deny him this is to refuse to take him seriously at the one place where he wanted to stand. Before proceeding to his *theology* of the demonic, we would do well to recognize the elements of his times which he definitely shared with his predecessors and contemporaries. We also need to note the strong role that personal experience played in his theology. In this way we may sift the enduring and pertinent from the time-conditioned in his thought.

I Zeitgeist and Personal Experience

The most direct access to both the question of the relationship of Luther to his milieu and the role of experience in his theology is gained by looking at what Luther called *Anfechtung*. While this term is sometimes translated as "temptation" (*Versuchung*), it actually has no real English equivalent. Its root means "assail," "combat," "bodily struggle." Thus "temptation" is too weak and misleading a translation for Luther's sense of *Anfechtung*. Professor Bainton defines *Anfechtung* as "all the doubt, turmoil, pang, tremor, panic, despair, desolation and desperation which invade the spirit of man." [9] For Luther, *Anfechtung* is the attack of God upon man; it is theocentric, whereas temptation is anthropocentric. It is interesting that one of the great influences on modern thought, Søren Kierkegaard, makes a similar distinction: "*Anfechtung* is in the sphere of the God-relationship what temptation is in the ethical sphere . . . the orientation of the individual is also different in the two cases. In temptation, it is the lower that tempts; in *Anfechtung* it is the higher; in temptation, it is the lower that allures the individual, in *Anfechtung* it is the higher that, as if jealous of the

individual, tries to frighten him back." [10] The horror of this con-
frontation by the Holy is so great that Luther exclaims that it can
turn a man to ashes. The Holy God relates to sinful man who is
egocentric, proud and unbelieving, as the Judge who condemns and
kills in order to give new life. This is radically presented in
Luther's exposition of Psalm 117:

> God's faithfulness and truth must always first become a great lie be-
> fore it becomes the truth. The world calls this truth heresy. And we,
> too, are constantly tempted to believe that God would abandon us
> and not keep his Word; and in our hearts he begins to become a liar.
> In short, God cannot be God unless he first becomes a devil. We
> cannot go to heaven unless we first go to hell. We cannot become
> God's children until we first become the children of the devil. All
> that God speaks and does the devil has to speak and do first.[11]

This is definitely not a continuation of medieval superstition and
demonology even though Luther did share his contemporaries'
ability to see the supernatural break into the natural in the form of
magic, demons, witches and spirits. "The angels are very close to
us . . . the devils, too, are very near us . . . there are many demons
in the woods, water, swamps and deserted places . . . others are in
dense clouds and cause storms, lightning, thunder, and hail and
poison the air." [12]

However, *Anfechtung* is so severe that troublesome demons pale
into child's play by comparison. Here the devil is no longer as the
artists have portrayed him—black and smoky with claws.[13] Here
man has to do with God. *Anfechtung* holds such terror because the
experience is theocentric. It is God who has the power to reject
man, to give him over to sin, death, and the devil. The devil himself does not have this power or independence. Thus Luther can
laugh at the medieval devil and chase him away with a fart! [14] The
demonic is demonic precisely because it is the "mask of God." In
a very real, experiential way for Luther, God may hide himself
from man, leave man on his own, and, even worse, then attack
man! "Therefore faith is not a laughable, cold quality that snores
and is idle in the heart. No, it is agitated and harassed by horrible
trials concerning the nothingness and vanity of the divine promises." [15] The biblical heroes vividly illustrated this for Luther. For
example, Jonah in the fish's belly looked death in the face; his *An-
fechtungen* included the hellish aspects of eternal damnation,
eternal anxiety, distress, eternal death, fear and despair.[16]

. . . God does not act according to our wish when he governs according to his goodness, wisdom, etc. Then we do not understand; for we think God does not know us and does not want to concern himself with or think about the outcome of our trial. That is the way reason judges. . . . Therefore we should know that God hides himself under the form of the worst devil. This teaches us that the goodness, mercy, and power of God cannot be grasped by speculation, but must be understood on the basis of experience.[17]

When God works, he turns his face away at first and seems to be the devil, not God. . . . (God says) ". . . I shall act in such a way that it will seem to you that some fool has done this, not God. You must see my back, not my face. You must not see my works and my counsels with which I am fashioning and refashioning you according to my good pleasure. It should seem foolish to you. But you will not accept and understand these things in any other way than if they were death and the devil himself." [18]

From this brief look at Luther's experience of *Anfechtung* we can begin to see that for Luther the demonic is only possible with the Holy; there is no devil without God. Although there are certainly the traditional ontological elements present in this view, this is primarily a theological position. Evil and the demonic are not the nether end of the chain of being but are paradoxically present in the Holy, in God himself. The God who gives himself to man, also withholds himself, hides himself, and masks himself from man. All human attempts to penetrate this mask only make it more impenetrable and awesome, for God is not passive but always leads, rules, and directs.[19] To see the naked God, God as he is in himself, is to be smitten by terror and crushed and led into despair by Satan. "You cannot nakedly associate with his naked Godhead. But Christ is our way to God." [20]

We have seen that Luther's thought and speech does reflect elements of the medieval view of the devil, but that it also radically transcends the *Zeitgeist*. We have also seen that his personal experience of the Holy is integral to his view of the demonic. It now remains to show that this experience is not autonomous but is tied to the Scriptures; it is a theology of the demonic.

II Luther's Theology of the Demonic

It is no accident that Luther's understanding of the demonic is linked so intimately with his understanding of God, for his struggle for salvation was a rejection of all moralistic paths to God. His struggle for righteousness was a struggle against God himself. That is, in his monastic search for a "gracious God" Luther found himself more estranged from God the more he strove to please God. God appeared as over against him to the extent of incorporating demonic traits in his wrath. Later in his life, Luther recalled that when he was in *Anfechtung*, his confessor would say to him, " 'You are a fool. God is not incensed against you, but you are incensed against God. God is not angry with you, but you are angry with God.' " [21] And in his autobiographical reflections he says:

> Though I lived as a monk without reproach, I felt that I was a sinner before God with an extremely disturbed conscience. I could not believe that he was placated by my satisfactions. I did not love, yes, I hated the righteous God who punishes sinners, and secretly, if not blasphemously, certainly murmuring greatly, I was angry with God . . . I raged with a fierce and troubled conscience. Nevertheless I beat importunately upon Paul at that place, most ardently desiring to know what St. Paul wanted.[22]

The experience of God's wrath is so strong that it appears in the moment as ultimate, demonic destruction. Luther could wish that "God had never revealed the gospel" because this angry, judging, condemning God placed him in "death and hell." [23] It was out of this existential orientation that Luther could say, "As you believe him, so you have him." "If you believe that God is wrathful, you will certainly have him wrathful and hostile to you. But this will be a demonic, idolatrous, and perverse thought, because God is served if you fear him and grasp Christ as the object of mercy." [24]

It was through exhaustive study of the Scripture, "meditating day and night," that Luther "began to understand that the righteousness of God is that by which the righteous lives by a gift of God, namely by faith. . . . The righteousness of God is revealed by the gospel; namely, the passive righteousness with which merciful God justifies us by faith; as it is written, 'He who through faith is righteous shall live.' " [25] This liberation allows Luther to see the Scriptures in an entirely new light, and now the work of God appears as what God does in us, *i.e.*, the power of God makes us strong, the wisdom of God makes us wise, etc.[26] The Word, then, is the place where God meets man and resolves the ambiguity of the divine and the demonic. It should be noted here that for Luther the Word of God is not confined to words. It is primarily Christ, secondarily the preached Word, and thirdly the Scriptures. For Luther it is crucial that God never be approached apart from Christ and the Scriptures.

> . . . Inexperienced monks rise into heaven with their speculations and think about God as he is in himself. From this absolute God everyone should flee who does not want to perish, because human nature and the absolute God . . . are the bitterest of enemies . . . We must take hold of this God, not naked but clothed and revealed in his Word; otherwise certain despair will crush us. . . . Therefore Satan is busy day and night, making us run to the naked God so that we forget his promises and blessing shown in Christ and think about God and judgment of God. When this happens, we utterly perish and fall into despair.[27]

Thus it is only in Christ that God is revealed as God and the devil as the devil. Only in Christ is it possible to see through the apparent dreadfulness of God and the pretense of Satan. Only in Christ is it clear that God is not the devil and that the devil is not God. Thus the devil's entire work is to mask the revealed God in Christ. In Luther's thought, the work of the devil is always "against Christ."[28] ". . . It is difficult for us believers to break through; for all the fury of Satan is devoted to this one thing, namely, that he may separate us from the Word, and that we, exhausted and broken either by the multitude or the long duration of our tribulations, may forsake and reject the Word."[29] Misunderstanding the Word of God "is due to the malice of Satan, who sits enthroned in our weakness, resisting the Word of God."[30]

Although Jesus Christ resolves the ambiguity of God and Satan, this does not mean that the tension-filled dialectic of Satan as the Mask of God and as the Prince of Lies is thereby dissolved. The work of God and the work of Satan are to be seen as one, yet also to be distinguished. Satan is the mask of God's wrath, the instrument by which God brings man to despair of himself in order that he may trust in Christ. There is no Manichaean dualism in Luther, for in every aspect of life and death it is God with whom man must deal. Here, paradoxically, is the comfort of the gospel, for even when confronted by suffering and death it is God himself who is dealing with us. This God is not arbitrarily angry or friendly, but is known through Jesus Christ to be consistently merciful, even in his attacks. When God launches an attack on man he does it in order to save man by driving him into God's arms. But Satan's goal is to tear a man completely loose from God by causing him to despair completely of the forgiveness of sins.

> ". . . Satan kills, the Law accuses; and yet the Scriptures attribute both of these to God." This is the reason: so that we might be preserved in the article of our Creed that there is only one God, lest with the Manichaeans we make more gods. . . . But God wants us, whether in pleasant or adverse circumstances, to have confidence in him alone. . . . So God is good, righteous and merciful even when he strikes. Whoever does not believe this departs from the unity of the faith that God is one, and he imagines another god for himself, who is inconstant, sometimes good and sometimes bad. But it is an outstanding gift of the Holy Spirit to believe that when God sends evil, he is still gracious and merciful.[31]

On the other hand, the devil "can tolerate neither the Word of God nor those who keep and teach it. He besets them in life and death." The devil's attacks are so great that "the wretched conscience believes that God, the devil, death, sin, hell and all creatures are one and have united as its eternal and relentless enemy. Neither the Turk nor the emperor can ever storm a city with such power as the devil uses in attacking a conscience." After enumerating how the devil disguises man's real sin of unbelief and frightens man with man's own best works, Luther says, "But who can list all the tricks by which the devil invokes sin, death, and hell? This is his trade. He has been at it for more than five thousand years, and he is a past master at it." Man's only hope is to turn away from self and cling to the hand of God, saying: " 'Devil, what are you fighting? If you try to denounce my good works and my holiness before God, why I have none. My strength is not my own; the Lord is my strength. You can't squeeze blood out of a turnip! If you try to prosecute my sins, I have none of those, either. Here is God's strength—prosecute it until you have had enough. I know absolutely nothing about either sins or holiness in me. I know nothing whatever except God's power in me.' " [32]

A comfort to Luther when confronted by the devil is to remember the distinction between law and gospel. The theological use of the law is to convince man of sin so that he no longer depends upon himself, but turns to the gospel which is the forgiveness of sins. Thus just because one is a sinner does not mean he needs to deny the gospel. Just the contrary! The forgiveness of sins covers all. With this in mind Luther can say to the devil, "Kiss my backside."

> The devil turns the Word upside down. If one sticks to the law, one is lost. A good conscience won't set one free, but the distinction [between law and gospel] will. So you should say, "The Word is twofold, on the one hand terrifying and on the other comforting." Here Satan objects, "But God says you are damned because you don't keep the law." I respond, "God also says that I shall live." His mercy is greater than sin, and life is stronger than death.[33]

In other words, to try to beat Satan on his own ground, by fulfilling the law and creating one's own life out of good works, will only lead to despair and death. Life comes from acceptance; it is the gift of God which is stronger than death.

Along with this motif of law and gospel, Luther speaks of God's activity in terms of his "alien work" and his "proper work." God uses Satan for his "alien work" in order to accomplish his "proper work," *i.e.*, he kills in order to make alive, he destroys dependence upon works so that man may live free of repression and anxiety. Satan, however, attempts to use God's "alien work" to totally destroy life itself. So Luther can regard Satan as both the instrument and enemy of God. He is both used and opposed by God.[34]

This strong theocentric emphasis of Luther's thought—which equates God's wrath with the devil, demonic powers, sin, death, and the law—raises the question of Luther's christology. Christ's work is a battle against the demonic powers used by God. The "monsters" against which Christ wages battle are understood theocentrically.

> Thus the curse, which is the divine wrath against the whole world, has the same conflict with the blessing—that is, with the eternal grace and mercy of God in Christ. Therefore the curse clashes with the blessing and wants to damn it and annihilate it. But it cannot. . . . Therefore Christ, who is the divine Power, Righteousness, Blessing, Grace, and Life, conquers and destroys these monsters—sin, death, and the curse—without weapons or battle, in His own body and in Himself . . .[35]

Christ's personal victory over the demonic powers does not mean that they are no longer present, but that they have lost their power in the presence of Christ. The reality of his victory is a spatial one, *i.e.*, where he is *present*, rather than a temporal one, *i.e.*, a metaphysical change in the world *since* Good Friday and Easter. The demonic powers, the law, the wrath of God still exist, but are overcome for those to whom Christ is present through faith.

> Let no one undertake to be saved through the faith or works of someone else. Yes, you cannot be saved through the faith and work of Mary or even of Christ himself without your own faith. . . . No alien faith or work is of any use at all, even if it is Christ's who is the Savior of the whole world; his benefits and his help are of no use to you unless you believe and are enlightened.[36]

Thus Christ's battle goes on in the Church and in the individual Christian. In principle, sin, death, the Devil, the demonic powers, and the wrath of God are conquered by Christ, but empirically they continue to exercise their power where Christ does not rule. Christ's struggle is continued constantly in every Christian, who is always in this life both sinner and righteous at the same time. The Christian is a sinner when he depends on himself, for then God's wrath strikes his conscience. But he is righteous and overcomes God's wrath when he grasps Christ in faith. This faith in Christ frees man from the demonic powers and makes him a free lord of all things. Nothing can do him any harm, but in fact serves him in obtaining salvation. Of course, Luther says, ordinary experience contradicts this, for everyone suffers and must die. Even Christ himself suffered evil and death. Nevertheless ". . . There is nothing so good and nothing so evil but that it shall work together for the good, if only I believe. Yes, since faith alone suffices for salvation, I need nothing except faith exercising the power and dominion of its own liberty. Lo, this is the inestimable power and liberty of Christians." [37]

This freedom is freedom from the wrath of God. This is the greatest freedom there is; for Christ, by satisfying God's wrath, has freed man from sin, death, the devil, hell and the law. The accusation of the law and the terror of sin can no longer plunge the believer into despair.[38] We do not have the space here to replay the 19th-century controversey between Albrecht Ritschl and Theodosius Harnack over whether Christ's work was rendered to the demonic powers or to God, a controversy renewed more recently by the work of Gustav Aulen.[39] But we do note that Luther often did describe Christ's work as a struggle with demonic powers and that these powers have authority only through God's wrath. Thus

Christ's primary work is stilling God's wrath which therefore deprives the demonic of its authority. Once more we come to assert that Luther's understanding of the demonic is a theological—indeed, a theocentric—understanding.

III Conclusions

On the basis of our discussion of Luther's theology of the demonic we may draw conclusions which hopefully will provide clues to our own experience, as well as that of the Reformers. First, while Luther remained in many ways in his medieval context, he nevertheless departed from it radically enough to begin the process of demythologizing the devil and the demonic. Second, his understanding of the demonic as the alienation from God and the world as well as the masking of God's grace, clarifies his bitter struggle against all heresy. Third, his persistent theological orientation rejected all attempts to equate God with the good and the demonic with the bad. This stands against all moralistic and ascetic impulses which appeared in other Reformers and have persisted, often in secularized form, down to our own day.

Luther's departure from the medieval depiction of the devil leads to what we may call the "demythologization" of the demonic. He sees no typical *Gestalt* of the devil; in fact he frequently makes no satanic impression at all but rather appears as the "angel of light." The devil and demonic are within us—sin and conscience are the devils which plague us. "But Christ has conquered these two monsters and trodden them underfoot, both in this age and the age to come." [40] Hans-Martin Barth points to the following quotes to illustrate this: "The devil or your heart will speak to you." . . . "How vehemently the world would be conformed to hell." And, "There is no world outside us." Thus "we have no greater enemy than ourselves." [41] Certainly the devil is characterized as a personal power through the law and wrath of God, but he is also related to the flesh and the world and thus depersonalized.

This demythologization of the devil is what allows Luther to call particular heretics the devil. "Those who persecute the truth are known as the incarnation of the devil." [42] Luther connects his opponents with the devil not as a means of propaganda but out of the theological perspective that heresy serves to hide and withhold the grace of God from men. Here heresy is not merely a misfortunate turn in the path of the history of the Church; it is rather the conscious choice of a deviant direction. Heresy is the attempt to split, to divide by elevating one element to divine status to the exclusion of the whole. The theologian who equates his particular theology with God is, in Tillich's terms, elevating the conditional to the unconditional.[43] The struggle to "protect" and manifest the work of God makes the heretic prey to his own demonic distortions. This invariably is expressed in legalistic and moralistic forms. Grace alone is displaced by the law, and thus once again man is faced by the wrath of God. It is because of these legalistic and ascetic developments in Luther's contemporary Reformers, Andreas Karlstadt and Thomas Müntzer, that he called them the incarnation of the devil. In Luther's eyes it was Thomas Müntzer who most overtly confused the gospel with the wrath of God. Müntzer was convinced that the righteous would usher in the kingdom of God with the sword, and that all godless should and would be put to death. Müntzer's self-consciousness of being the "hammer of God" and the "sword of Gideon" [44] is in marked contrast to Luther's self-assessment that "we are beggars all." [45] For Luther the political and theological categories of righteousness must always be distinguished. The former is concerned with fulfilling laws and constructing society; the latter is the acceptance of the forgiveness of sins which cannot be earned. For Müntzer this distinction is obliterated and human society is to be forced to be as perfect as God is perfect. The theological understanding of righteousness is transmuted to moral-political purity. Müntzer's program was ended by his execution for being a leader of the Peasants' War.

Karlstadt's concern was not so much to establish the Kingdom of God on earth as it was to purify the church. Any and all possibilities of idolatry must be removed; if the people did not understand the reason for this or did not willingly comply, then those who rightly understood the gospel must take the lead. So Karlstadt was a leader in the riots and disturbances in Wittenberg in 1521–22 during Luther's absence. It was for this orientation that Hermann Barge subtitled the second volume of his study of Karlstadt, "Karlstadt as the pioneer of lay-Christian Puritanism." [46] Luther's restoration of order to Wittenberg impelled Karlstadt to seek purity on the personal rather than the ecclesiastical level to the extent that he renounced his academic degrees and title and for a while attempted to live as a peasant. Both Müntzer and Karlstadt were denounced by Luther because in one way or another they insisted on coercing the Kingdom of God. Luther, on the contrary, was content to preach the gospel, drink good Wittenberg beer, and let God work out his purposes in history. To a revolutionary, Luther was a failure because he did not take his work seriously. From Luther's point of view only God may be taken seriously; man's own work is always penultimate.

Paradoxically, it might seem, it was precisely Luther's understanding of the numinous character of God, his holiness and wrath, which prohibited any attempt to equate himself or his work with God. Luther always insisted both before and after the Peasants' War that the world may not be governed by the gospel. His theme, "Let God be God" is his way of allowing man to be man, *i.e.*, to be human rather than prey to the demonic urge to play God. Because Luther took God rather than man seriously, he was free to see man and the devil as penultimates. He could laugh at the devil. Karlstadt and Müntzer could not. He could appreciate and thoroughly enjoy the natural and the human, but Karlstadt and Müntzer could not. For example, Luther was shocked that Müntzer did not rejoice in the birth of his son,[47] and in the face of the tragedy of the Peasants' War, Luther could marry his Katy to spite his enemies.[48] This was not callousness, but a distinction between the ultimate and the penultimate. Because of his theology, eros and joy were by no means alien to Luther. In this Luther may have been far more radical, even revolutionary, than Müntzer and Karlstadt, for love is an explosive force. It is not without interest here that totalitarian and tyrannical political systems are puritanical. Luther's advice to a friend suffering from depression and despair also illustrates his ordering of priorities. He counsels hearing the gospel and then, "Having been taught by experience, I can say how you ought to restore your spirit when you suffer from spiritual depression. When you are assailed by gloom, despair, or a troubled conscience you should eat, drink and talk with others. If you can find help for yourself by thinking of a girl, do so." [49]

Perhaps the greatest contribution to our experience of the demonic that Luther's theology makes is his linking of the demonic to the wrath of God. This is a corrective to what Weber called the "disenchantment of the world," [50] *i.e.*, the radical separation of creation from Creator which has issued in alienation and secularism. Protestantism purged the medieval world of sacred and demonic beings and forces. As we have already suggested, Luther himself began the "demythologization" of the demonic. Perhaps "remythologize" would be a better term; for Luther did not banish the demonic; he placed it in the wrath of God. It was the Reformers who absolutized the transcendence of God to the extent that "the finite is not capable of the infinite" that began the process of divesting the world of what Otto called the "numinous." The world that cannot bear the infinite, the sacred, is closed to it. Man is thrown back upon himself, alienated and alone. Certainly Reformers such as Karlstadt, Müntzer, Zwingli, and Calvin were not intent upon creating alienation and puritanical loneliness. They never tired of emphasizing the Word of God to man. But this Word was really the "Word alone." In time this thread connecting God and man snapped under the weight of the Enlightenment and critical reason, technology and revolution. The cry arose that God was dead, or if not dead, then left standing outside the world presumably as lonely as his creatures encapsuled within it. When the creation no longer refracted the demonic, it also no longer carried the sacred. Here, of course, we are talking of that progressive narrowing of the Word down to the written words of the Bible, that intellectualizing of life which has alienated us from nature and things which also bear the wrath and grace of God. This process was reflected in all realms of Protestant experience. One example easily visible is that of church architecture where unstained glass allows light to enter which is neither broken nor glorified by profound colors; where the "purity" of white (which really is no color at all) replaces the symbol of transcendence expressed by gold. The Reformers other than Luther strove to purify the church by removing as much medieval art as possible. A first step on the way to thinking that cleanliness was somehow close to godliness.

Luther's appreciation of creation is well known [51] and was the source of bitter conflict not only with Karlstadt but also, later, in the eucharistic controversies with Zwingli. Not only did Luther refuse to denude the church of music, stained glass, vestments, and the crucifix but, more importantly, he always emphasized the centrality of the sacraments, the visible Word. He strongly opposed the Reformed position that the "finite is not capable of carrying the infinite." Bread and wine were not merely stimulants for the memory of Christ; they are the bearers of Christ's real presence. This is misunderstood if it is seen only as a self-serving defense of his own theology or as a remnant of medieval magic. Behind Luther's insistence on the Real Presence in the eucharist was the conviction that the depth and mystery of the Holy worked in, with, and under the material of this world. Luther rejected transubstantiation because he understood this as an identification of the Holy with the medium of revelation, but he nevertheless continued to insist that the finite may bear the infinite. The other Reformers struggled so successfully against the possibility of idolatry that the Holy was transformed into the morally good, and righteousness was given ascetic connotations. The logical and historical outcome of this was to approximate the Holy to moral perfection and the demonic to the unclean. This is stated succinctly by Tillich:

> Fear of the demonic permeates Calvin's doctrine of divine holiness. An almost neurotic anxiety about the unclean develops in later Calvinism. The word "Puritan" is most indicative of this trend. The holy is the clean; cleanliness becomes holiness. This means the end of the numinous character of the holy. The *tremendum* becomes fear of the law and judgment; the *fascinosum* becomes the pride of self-control and repression.[52]

Contemporary phenomena such as glossalalia, countercultural returns to "primitive" religion and life-style, and the rise of cults such as astrology and satanism may be indications of the poverty of a theology which in its zeal to repress the demonic has only succeeded in freeing the demonic for "independent existence." It was Luther's insight that only when the demonic is identical with the wrath of God is there hope that the demonic will be overcome, for the work of Christ satisfies the wrath of God. Luther's insight that the holy expresses itself through the unholy, the infinite through the finite, God through creation, may provide us with the possibility of once more seeing life in its divine-demonic ambiguity, and even more importantly, to be able to accept this tension-filled dynamic of life.

NOTES

In the notes that follow, these two abbreviations will be used in the interests of clarity and conserving space.

WA=D. *Martin Luthers Werke,* Kritische Gesamtausgabe, Weimar, 1883ff. The numbers following WA refer to volume, page, and line numbers.

LW=*Luther's Works,* Philadelphia/St. Louis, 1958ff.

1. Rudolf Otto, *The Idea of the Holy,* trans. J. W. Harvey (New York: Oxford University Press, 1923; paperback reprint 1971), p. 99.
2. Paul Tillich, *Systematic Theology,* I (Chicago: University of Chicago Press, 1953), pp. 216ff.

3. WA 5, 163, 28–29. Operationes in Psalmos, 1518–21; In his Preface to the German edition of his works, Luther says that *Anfechtung* "is the touchstone which teaches you not only to know and understand, but also to experience how right, how true, how sweet, how lovely, how mighty, how comforting God's Word is, wisdom beyond all wisdom. . . . For as soon as God's Word takes root and grows in you, the devil will harry you and make a real doctor out of you, and by his assaults will teach you to seek and love God's Word." LW 34, 286f; 1539.

4. See E. G. Schwiebert, *Luther and his Times* (St. Louis: Concordia, 1950), pp. 518–19; Heinrich Boehmer, *Martin Luther: Road to Reformation* (New York: Meridian Books), p. 430.

5. For the history of Catholic polemics against Luther, see Adolf Herte, *Das katholische Lutherbild im Bann der Lutherkommentare des Cochlaus*, 3 vols., Munster I.W., 1943. For more recent positive Catholic interpretations, see Jared Wicks, ed., *Catholic Scholars Dialogue with Luther* (Chicago: Loyola University Press, 1970).

6. Erik Erikson, *Young Man Luther* (New York: Norton, 1958).

7. Norman O. Brown, *Life Against Death* (New York: Vintage Books, 1959).

8. *Ibid.*, p. 209.

9. *Here I Stand* (Nashville: Abingdon Press, 1950), p. 42. Quoted by C. Warren Hovland, *"Anfechtung* in Luther's Biblical Exegesis," p. 56, in Franklin Littell, ed., *Reformation Studies, Sixteen Essays in Honor of Roland H. Bainton* (Richmond: John Knox, 1962).

10. *Concluding Unscientific Postscript to the Philosophical Fragments* (Princeton: Princeton University Press, 1941), p. 410. Quoted by Hovland, *ibid.*, p. 55.

11. LW 14, 31; Commentary on Psalm 117, 1530.

12. LW 54, 172; Table Talk. See also pp. 188, 279, 241, 298.

13. WA 34II, 361, 29ff.; Epistola Ephesi. VI, 1531.

14. LW 54, 16 & 78, Table Talk; WA TR 1, 48, 11 & 205, 1: "mit ein furtz."

15. LW 5, 205; Lectures on Genesis, 1541–42.

16. WA 19, 218, 5–219, 11; Der Prophet Jona Ausgelegt, 1526.

17. LW 7, 175; Lectures on Genesis, 1544.

18. LW 7, 103–104.

19. LW 7, 104.

20. LW 16, 54f. Lectures on Isaiah, 1528.

21. LW 54, 15. Table Talk.

22. LW 34, 336–37; Preface to the Complete Edition of Luther's Latin Writings, 1545.

23. LW 5, 158.

24. LW 12, 322; Psalm 51, 1538. See also Paul Tillich, *Systematic Theology*, II (Chicago: University of Chicago Press, 1959), p. 77.

25. LW 34, 337.

26. *Loc cit.*

27. LW 12, 312.

28. See Hans-Martin Barth, "Zur inneren Entwicklung von Luthers Teufelsglauben" *Kerygma und Dogma* 13 (1967), 201–211, p. 201.

29. LW 5, 234.

30. LW 33, 100; The Bondage of the Will, 1525.
31. LW 12, 373–74; See also LW 33, 175–78.
32. LW 14, 84–85; Commentary on Psalm 118, 1530.
33. LW 54, 106; Table Talk.
34. LW 14, 335; Commentary on Psalm 2, 1518.
35. LW 26, 281–82; Lectures on Galatians, 1535.
36. WA 10III, 306, 308; Sermon von dem Tauben und Stummen, 1522.
37. LW 31, 354f.; The Freedom of a Christian, 1520.
38. LW 27, 4f.; Lectures on Galatians, 1535.
39. See Paul Althaus, *The Theology of Martin Luther*, trans. R. C. Schultz (Philadelphia: Fortress Press, 1966), pp. 218ff.; Ian Siggins, *Martin Luther's Doctrine of Christ* (New Haven & London: Yale, 1970); Gustaf Aulen, *Christus Victor* (London: SPCK, 1945).
40. LW 26, 26.
41. WA 5, 172, 34; Operationes in Psalmos, 1519ff. WA 1, 38f.; Sermon, 1514. WA 1, 14, 28; Sermon, 1512. WA 2, 105, 3; Auslegung deutsch des Vaterunsers, 1519. Barth, *op. cit.*, p. 209.
42. WA 37, 503, 30; Predigt, 1534.
43. Tillich, *Systematic Theology*, I, *op. cit.*, p. 140.
44. See for example Müntzer's "Sermon Before the Princes," in *Spiritual and Anabaptist Writers*, ed. and trans. G. H. Williams (Philadelphia: Westminster Press, 1957), and the essay by Gordon Rupp on Müntzer in his *Patterns of Reformation* (Philadelphia: Fortress Press, 1969).
45. LW 54, 476; Table Talk.
46. Hermann Barge, *Andreas Bodenstein von Karlstadt*, 2 vols., Leipzig, 1905; reprint 1968. See also Rupp's essay on Karlstadt in *Patterns of Reformation, op. cit.*
47. "Formerly the monks made senseless logs and stones out of men, and Satan wanted the special commendation to be published about his saints that they were not disturbed by affections of any kind, were stolid men, and Stoics seven times over. . . . A few years ago we saw schismatic spirits trying to introduce apathy of this kind into the church. Müntzer strove to express it in his life and ways as outstanding sanctity. For when the birth of a son was announced to him, he stood before the altar as if he were deaf and dumb. . . . Afterwards he boasted that his nature was completely changed and slain. This was really fanaticism far worse than the delirium of the Stoics. For God wants nature to be preserved, not abolished." LW 7, 261; Lectures on Genesis, 1544.
48. See Gordon Rupp, *The Righteousness of God: Luther Studies* (New York: Philosophical Library, 1953), p. 351.
49. LW 54, 17f.
50. Max Weber, *The Protestant Ethic and the Spirit of Capitalism* (New York: Scribner's, 1958), pp. 105, 117, 149. See also, Peter Berger, *The Sacred Canopy* (New York: Doubleday Anchor, 1967), chapter 5.
51. See, for example, Roland Bainton's essay, "Luther on Birds, Dogs, and Babies," in *Luther Today*, Decorah, Iowa, 1957.
52. Paul Tillich, *Systematic Theology*, I (Chicago: University of Chicago Press, 1953), pp. 216–17.

THE AFFABLE PRIEST:
AN ESSAY IN THE FORM OF FICTION

> "When at thirty, I want to 'dash the cup to the ground', wherever I may be I'll come to have one more talk with you, even though it were from America, you may be sure of that. I'll come on purpose. It will be very interesting to have a look at you, to see what you'll be by that time."
> —from "The Grand Inquisitor,"
> *The Brothers Karamazov.*

"YOU'VE BEEN HAUNTED, haven't you, ever since I warned you there would be another conversation, even in America! You thought this would protect you, being here. But, even though we shortened our name (to that amicable abbreviation 'Karam' !), remember, we are brothers, the two of us, and no one can protect himself from his brother. He may keep himself busy, fill his mind with details or even borrow a new set of ideals or cultural amalgamations, but his brother knows him as he is, humanly, by blood, by memory, by envy or by spite. Irritations as well as love live on to remind us we are brothers.

"You remember the last time we talked—in Russia—we spoke of 'freedom' then, and I placed its possession on the purple lips of a gloomy ninety-year-old priestly relic of the Inquisition in beloved suffering Spain, the natural home of saints and devil's advocates, the tenebrous nest constructed by the followers of Mecca and Jerusalem. The devil in the Gospels was an august tempter of the divine self in the desert. The Middle Ages mistakenly portrayed him as ugly, when he was, in fact, beautiful, capable of attracting and moving all but the divine. And the Modern World insists that, if he is not reduced to myth, he at least be in some sense eccentric, when, in fact, he is most appealing and affective to the conventionally normal among us. In the Koran, or at least in the works of its more mystical commentators, Satan was a lover of God who couldn't share Him with man nor modify his prior conception of love to include a creature less worthy, in his own mind, than himself. He was a jealous lover. The truly satanic in both versions lies in our latent possessiveness aroused to the surface by the appearance of something different from ourselves that we did not create or plan for or imagine possible, and which we can neither accommodate nor reverse. In historical fusion they produced inquisitions and unconscionable sufferings. The inquisitor was a failed dialogist grown old in talking only to himself, and underneath it all a failed intimate of God. You told me then that no such priest existed and I assured you it was just a 'dream.'

"You are silent. You had more protest in you then in Russia. It was because my thoughts were dark and you, my youngest brother, were full of joy and wanted only light. Yet then you kissed me. Compassion still belonged to us, and we could still call out to compassion without fear of embarrassment. But here we are all anxiously moving; everyone carries in him the desire to be quickly disinvolved or divorced. Also, you seem to have lost that joy, as I have lost the dark inquisitor. Things have changed. Our positions may even have become reversed. If we could only listen well enough to find out how—or why. You don't protest my argument (it doesn't even seem to you to be one), nor do I think you will have the love to kiss me on the lips when I am through. You see, you—the official 'Christian' of what is left of our family—have been made to believe that kissing brothers is not done. Perhaps it too was a scandal, yet I used to think that all the rest of our old life was a scandal and that this was one of the few precious things of decency. Perhaps both of us in our compromised positions can no longer make distinctions. The world is just as dark and palpitating on the edge of a disaster as before, but we are 'free' of inner dialogue, of deeper irritation; we are lost in dedication to our good intentions. The saint and devil's advocate are both deceived. Each is without a constituency. A history which has no argument for temptation or miracle, which circulates, exchanging and discarding, under the very terms of the three temptations, intangible freedom, has made both obsolete.

"I am not surprised that you are silent—'prudent,' you would say—nor that I talk on, for I was always the preacher, irreligious perhaps because I knew that I, without belief, could make up better sermons than official priests; and you, always the patient, obedient seminarian. I am so even here in a private room in a mental institution, which is, in fact, the only place we could gain admission, you and I, into this well-fortified country of America, for our discussion. No one is burned here for his heresy, except in brief periods of official aberration; he is either quietly unrepresented or put under temporary observation. Not even a crime can claim a right to permanence. And that makes our new country indeed more charitable than our old one. More charitable, when no one can be legally denied a life based on the hope of change.

"Oh, don't move forward in your chair like that; I am not questioning our charity or change and, even less, our improvement on the old; I am just 'talking,' as I always do. Perhaps I still have something lingering in me of a 'foreign' outlook. I realize the value to some of 'roots' or of other, more primitive, standards of perception. It would seem that I, the rationalist, the atheist, am defending here what men of faith defended in the Old World. For even the saints can't remember what took place a year or two ago and misunderstand what happens elsewhere. To search too much through memory, it seems, is a lack of charity, since no one else recalls. We have our private memories, which do no general harm, and keep our suffering to ourselves or under the care of specialists. We keep our dialogues confined to one form or another of mental institution.

"Yet still *we* have our conversation. And it is because you and I know something is unfinished between us. I wanted to see if you had changed, and you wanted to prove that you still could be as simple and as good.

"We spoke of fear before—or, rather, I did, and you listened. Perhaps your silence means you are waiting for my story, my parable or 'dream,' to see if it is really fearful or if I'm just another private citizen, like all the others, or like you, whose revelation is no serious threat. You are silent, perhaps, because you know I can no longer evoke dark parables; you defy me with a patriotic confidence to evoke the absolutely dark thing that goes unattended or unassimilated however slowly into the general weal; you think I am imagining my cause for fear; you defy me to 'prove' it; you accept my status as a 'case.' I must admit our parables are also things of compromise. No tragedies, no great man's bearing of unendurable pain of his own causing. Our Oedipus is no longer Rex but Acadaemus, knowledgeable in facts and theories, but afraid to suffer the pain that goes with learning one is wrong. He is proud, but he is not yet a man. Our poor old dancing fool of a father, who called out with every loud desperate ingratiating gesture of his body and soul for his murderer to come forward in the night was more tragic, but is forgotten, like the last portion of our name. And so we think all sufferings can be handled legally or by technicians or by the family in consultation with the doctor, ending in agreement to deceive, to burden him, with no fear of other unknown suffering, to let him live his cancer or his madness out believing he is relatively well or sane. Isn't that the case? Isn't the one who guesses the truth an indescribably lonely man, unable to either give or gain a greater life from those closest to him, because he also has to deceive *them* that he and they are incapable of knowing or of becoming radical about the truth. For the sake of the common good everyone has to pretend he is (or actually to *be*) incapable of enduring the truth. The case himself lives in a void without communication; all relations are cut, human and divine, for how can the so-human God come to tell him that his meager suffering is a substitution for them, as His was long ago for all, if there is no one who wants to receive it or admit it, and no one through whom the simplest kind of love can come? Isn't it suffering, my brother, when no one can bear another's or his own suffering?

"You look uncomfortable. You are disagreeing, not in essentials but in details, perhaps. You are saying that from your knowledge as a young priest who makes his rounds through hospitals or visits the old in homes, our people are only too ready to pour out their miseries even over the slightest thing; they are even hypochondriacs; they can't bear any pain or disappointment; and so on. I hear you, from your first touches of experience, deciding you have seen enough to know. Your seminary instructors have taught you well: to learn to recognize that people whine, and as quickly as possible to comfort them so as not to waste too much of your time. All right, I won't go on about the seminary. I'll get to my story; I know you don't like listening to digressions. Or maybe you're afraid to disagree aloud for fear you'll 'set me off' talking about the past again . . .

"There is no grand inquisitor this time. No one who commands absolute obedience or orders Christ led off to a common prison where he redresses him with such didactic remarks as 'we don't need your return. We have taken on the freedom which men can't bear, yet which you unwisely gave them. We have improved upon your freedom, being more realistic. It is more viable now.' No, Christ passes now like any other stranger. No one arrests him. Demonstrators come and go, like demonstrations, pacified more or less by the embrace of official good intention, or discouraged into exhaustion or former indolence by the steady repetition of governmental indifference. No one is interested enough in Christ to recall his story. The freedom he gave is forgotten, being absorbed; he no longer can create a stir. And if one says that he is Christ, enough crazy followers will emerge and surround him, like all the other bizarre itinerant gurus, to get him into the ephemeral news where he can be commercialized and forgotten; or, if he persists, he will be taken *here* for observation, and will be merely visited at certain hours in the unreal world of institutions and then abandoned to the useless repetition of the things he has to say, even though it be *the* revelation. I know that specialists in this place have a way of getting one to compromise in order to regain admission to worlds that seem increasingly less real. They do it by training you to accept your beliefs only as *useful*, thereby convincing you that in order to communicate with people again for any length of time you must not expect or oblige them to take you seriously. Or, among the most enlightened specialists, there is a tendency to allow you to live your fantasy myth out to its end in complete belief, in hopes that the end will terminate your obvious schizophrenia. Every specialist realizes that extreme attachments can be dangerous, but as long as you, with the help of periodic consultation and pseudo-belief supports, can moderate them in public, you can lead a more or less useful life and not be a threat to society. For those of us who return here for long periods of time or who stay permanently, the specialists accept our story and forget *us* and simply make a place for us to live where we can read and amuse ourselves and be visited. We are looked upon with professional pity—one left to his silence, the other to his reasoned indignation, placed in such a way that (even though we might be brothers) we shall imagine one is being visited, the other is coming from outside to visit, retaining his perspective of normalcy, thereby not getting too close to each other in this new artificial context in which brothers do not touch or retain any deep or potentially fearful relationship of the past, but only stare and hold one-sided conversations respectively.

"But to continue with my story. There are still high priests, still Catholics, though not inquisitors; old but not gloomy. And the Jesuits, whom I indiscreetly criticized in the old days, are less ominous than helpful in suggesting ways of compromise. They are all cheerful and healthy; in fact, generous, athletic, liked. Even advisers to Presidents and overseas commanders. They don't like worried looks, though indeed they are as hard working as any fully employed citizen, if not more. They are doing what Christ said to do when fasting—not to show downcast looks—and many of them are doing it *without* fasting. But I am ahead of myself. I haven't physically created my high priest yet. That's a change, too. We must physically create something first, then try to accommodate it to a soul, not the reverse as in darker times.

"This priest is old. And you know why, because of the appearance of majesty—I am still attached to it; I am awed that it has survived, even if it hasn't the soul for tragedy, and also because I suspect that behind my 'dream' there is *an old compromiser*, to whom young dreamers have long since grown accustomed to responding and in whom they place their hopes, until he himself is almost forgotten, replaced by an aura—not an aura of sanctity or evil, but of power diffused through arrangements made behind the scenes with the right people and moderated by the warmth of geniality. He is the affable priest who serves for any time.

"I have dreamt of this priest as being tall and slightly stooped in his seventy-five-year-old shoulders, yet otherwise straight, robust in his walking, craggy in his face, no dragging of feet or ponderous suggestion of any weariness, so that he always seems to be entering a celebration being held in his honor and grows younger with applause and the sight of people he knows to share it with, people as ethnically ordinary as himself and as honest, on their feet at seventy-five or older when one of their kind enters the room with the same knowledgeable earthiness and enthusiasm for things in general. He also knows that they know all about his life—no secrets, no mystery. From the physical standpoint he may prefer a little privacy: for example, the backs of his hands are freckled where the skin seems to have decayed with age, but on gala occasions he rubs his hands with a soft bleaching cream, so that no one's eyes would be distracted or saddened by such unpleasant details. Besides, he believes in using the products which his 'lay' friends use (or even sell), within moderation of course, so as not to seem too distant. He even tells funny stories at dinner parties, and once, at a party given by the President, told about a priest who couldn't keep from breaking wind in mass. Everyone laughed; he was a natural, both as priest and as obliging jester. From the spiritual standpoint, he is well-known in the newspapers for his many social enterprises and good works, his building of Catholic schools and colleges, hospitals and old folks homes, as well as for his own personal struggles with disease and his prevailing over operations, struggles he takes publicly in stride, each one of which he comes through looking even younger. His light blue eyes, which his applauders know are shrewd in matters of the world, as shrewd as theirs ('He could have been a success in any line'), are nevertheless in the service of the Kingdom of God, watering when losses are to be shared, yet humorous when minimizing his own physical sufferings, and properly angry when descrying internal or external threats to national security. Part of his responsibility in accepting awards and giving testimonials to the politically important and preaching tolerance of minorities or supporting parishioners under investigation for one passing offense or another is the religious duty (during either celebration or crisis) of seeming jovial. His face crinkles easily in a smile, his voice cracks almost naturally— in fact, it is a coarse anyman's voice, a 'come, let us reason together' voice, that reminds people they are only human, not in any sense intellectually superior nor called to communicate subtle matters to one another in any form, and therefore should take nothing, especially not themselves, too seriously. And with his large enterprises involving money-raising campaigns for the missions overseas or for convents, monasteries, academic institutions, marriage counseling bureaus, clinics, Catholic mental institutions, convalescent homes, and the many other limbs of the large institutional body in some form or other, subject to his supervision and dependent on his support, he combines his natural inclination to go down to the level of the ordinary, to visit the sick, to build homes for orphans, and to lighten the minds of his industrious and studious and generally open-minded priests and sisters by taking them to athletic events to show the general public, and incidentally themselves, that they are also only human. He is in everyone's eyes, no less my own, I assure you, a friendly man, a saint in our context, open to all, unmysterious, possessive of his flock yet 'liberal,' someone who has reached the point of talking about the world naturally, it seems, unextremely either pro or con, peacefully, so that others imagine he is reflecting on the Next, without having to disturb their minds by serious reference to it. Some malcontents contend that he employs a double standard with the rich, that he waives for some the ban on contraception, leaving to others the challenge of avoiding 'sin'; but priests have always practiced such situational distinctions, and therefore he should not be criticized for anything so trivial as this. Indeed, if all leaders could achieve obedience by merely diverting people's attention away from the myriad of more serious spiritual problems to focus exclusively on something as simple as contraception, we might all live in a more peaceful world.

"Do you know a priest like the one in my 'dream'? Your neck seemed a little red with irritation. You see, my dream priest has trained you to be patient with everyone, but to let your blood rise to his defense if he is misinterpreted. You will recall in this respect, by way of analogy, my brother, the comment of a sister at the college where I taught briefly when I told her that my one questioning student had persisted in posing challenging questions one day instead of, like the others, taking what I said at face value. The sister said, 'Yes, she is immature, isn't she?' You see, certain areas are sacred and subject to 'authority,' even now. But it's just a dream I've been having. It's just a random chance if he resembles anyone you know. I promise you that I am creating a composite person and accommodating his body to a general soul. Don't you remember, our criticism is not meant to imply something about anyone in particular.

"But I've had the dream that this man, every bit as good as he seems, senses his experience is, for all his natural affability, a desert on which he inclines toward greater power; and, feeling that the entire country is his parish, he, out of the same shrewdness that taught him to respect the powerful, has set his mind assiduously on conquering the wider world with the same personal warmth. He has overcome fear of the unknown; he has replaced fear with charitable institutions, and has entered into amicable and harmonious arrangements with those more powerful institutions of the national government that are guided by the same intentions; and now, without declaring it as such, he is bent totally on a course of official 'love.' And this is where our earlier conversation resumes, around the theme of 'love' that expresses itself in the safeguarding of the general 'freedom': the taking on of what other souls, however remote they are from him in geographic or cultural space, cannot grasp satisfactorily on their own. He is the sum of his good intentions; he cannot be made to think that he is wrong.

"Doesn't it occur to you that I am particularly well situated to discuss this theme: I suffered under our father's lawlessness of freedom and the loving bonds he held us accountable to even unto his bankruptcy and outrageous death. And now, with all that has followed in the world, and our emigration here, our desire to get away from old ruins and injured memories and each other's suffering mouths speaking endlessly to each other's suffering mouths until one was almost mad. Forgive the pun, or is it irony? It would seem we had had enough of possessive authority not to let ourselves fall into the hands of another that promised to be good and seemed less openly bad. No, my brother, our mind is not free, and, finally, none of the old was lost; that is my fearful dream: that it all grew up again, our lawless father, our involvement in relentless crime, our agonies of unrest caused by our intense but helpless perceptions, the appearance among us of a bitter, unwanted son who kills more gratuitously than vengefully—all this relieved only by moments of a brother's love; all re-created again, but in a world where reason can be under observation and faith pacified, where brothers no longer, even if only for a moment, utterly reunite. Perhaps that would require too great a depth of freedom for man to bear, as either the grand inquisitor or the affable priest accepting the general state has shown. The shadows have gone, as have the fires that danced in them. But the priests are fundamentally the same, knowing now that without shadows it is more auspicious to smile. Hatred can be reserved by those distant few who resist his and his country's good intentions.

"Love—the kind divorced from conspicuous fear—all stance, all entertainment and desperate diversion—the kind designed to take the worried looks away—all pervasive, wired in, alive with accusations, defensive, wed to guilt it can't embrace—that is the root of my dream. And I see this old priest sitting at his light mahogany desk legislating love or calling those by phone who will. He says he loves the ones he knows enough to call; and he loves the untried strangers whose fears he says he doesn't understand. And when he has tried them and they resist him, he says he doesn't see his ensuing actions through any other eyes than love. He loves those among his own who call on him for aid and place their freedom in his care. By phone the state, from which he's separate as everyone knows, will do as much for one who asks for aid, at least in theory and with the help of contacts of well-placed people like himself. In his heart he wishes only, like it, to protect. He is patriot and priest, separated within but free from fear of contradiction. He knows that love is the only way to end aggression, foreign or domestic. God is love. Happiness is love. All feeling moves toward love. Love sanctifies even our machines; He only said, 'Go and preach in my name'—that is, in the Triunal Name, which is unified by Love. He left it up to His priests to work out the particulars.

"I am not only mad, but also perverse, my brother: I think the only demon to be exorcised from our world is the notion that our love is the answer to everyone's deepest desire to be free.

"I see your neck is reddening again, and I perceive it is because you think that I, by innuendo or insertion of the word *demon*, am impugning my old priest's motives. No, his motives are the highest. Or it is because you think that I, a layman and a rationalist, have no credentials or authority for investigating such a classified area of theological research? In any case, he's right about Christ: no such weapons as he now approves were mentioned by our saviour. And in our day we would not know—would we?—the religious basis on which Christ might make new pronouncements on such things. He said all he had a right to say. Love alone from his message has prevailed as being good for any time and causes the least fear of contradiction because of centuries of handling by realistic hearts and shrewd minds. Christ, that poor, humble person to whom a blind man called for cure because he had a reputation for free gifts and unpossessiveness—who preferred to bear wounds than to possess—who died while speaking of forgiveness rather than of achievements—who left us speaking of another world—Christ who allows this aged priest his human love of all mankind rather than deprive *him* of his freedom, which he has successfully translated into global concern.

"And I see the old priest in my dream visited by Christ in his chancery office by appointment. Christ awaits his turn among the other callers, among those seeking special dispensation or aid to build another institution. Finally he enters, and the craggy old priest rises and says in his down-to-earth voice, 'I am a man just like you and speak the same language.' The priest invites him to review the records and accounts of the number of missions and vocations and educational institutions, the lists of nuns who are good administrators, the signs of good relations with the state. He leans forward in his chair toward Christ and says, 'The state tells

me we are near victory; it sees the light at the end of the tunnel.'
He stands and throws his arm around Christ, offers him a cigar,
and tells him, 'Come again. I'm always glad to see you. Drop in
any time.' He slaps Christ on the back, confides how if he hadn't
become a priest, he might've become a gangster, and walks him to
the door, for he is busy, and tells his secretary to see him to the
elevator and to make sure the policeman outside the building finds
him a taxi.

"Yes, you redden now. You think, 'blasphemy!' You are saying
to yourself, 'Christ is God. The old priest would treat him differ-
ently from others, for He is to come in Glory!' But I am not ob-
jecting to the way the old priest treats him, I am only saying he
will come as poor and unneeded as he came before.

"My brother, do you think this priest of my dream, any more
than the dark and aged grand inquisitor, believes in God? He's
only more outgoing in his concern for mankind. No less does he
believe men unworthy of the freedom Christ has given them
than did that old dismal fossil of despair. Despair has only been
converted into a comfortable and, for most, agreeable way of life.
Only the inquisitor was more the way he seemed; my old likable
priest is what anyone wants him to be: he fills the void in the heart.
He is the subtler deceiver, for he lacks the uglier guile that comes
from knowing he has ceased to believe. He is the more outwardly
beautiful and approachable. Evil has gone from his memory and
from his consciousness as something belonging to an underdeveloped past. Only those who out of some perverseness or ignorance of their own still think about evil. Evil is no more. There
is only utility and love, which means expansive affability and which
all have agreed not to call aggrandizement.

"You see, I am not judging my old priest. He helps countless
millions of people every year and in a way takes their suffering
ungrudgingly. He is ready with his kindness and has good relations
with those of other faiths. The phone is in his hand to help. And if
he has someone whose brother is irascible or odd or didn't quite
work out after a period in society, he suggests a visit to the institution now concerned. He takes care of everything. He says to the
relatives, 'Go to see your brother. Let him know he's not forgotten,' just as he asks people to write to soldiers overseas. Let your
brother know, in short, that even in a mental institution he's still
part of the larger body and is not to feel abandoned. And if your

brother broods on the past or on his failure to meld with others or
dreams up fantasies, humor him; he's your brother; he's only mad.

"You are looking at your watch, my brother. I guess I took too
long with the tale, for you had only a little time to listen . . . like
everyone. But this was on your way, wasn't it, to other calls? Or
maybe out of your way? You missed your golf to come? And now
you have to get back to say your evening mass. Tell your fellow
priests—all of whom probably share each other's 'family worries,'
prudently, that is—that I sounded distracted as ever, dwelled on
dreams, as people are inclined to in these places, was even a touch
subversive, even extreme, but didn't actually say I'd 'lost my faith,'
though I did speak of wanting to be kissed on the lips, as in the old
days, to see if we were still brothers who could love . . . tell them
I was leaning toward scandal.

"Oh, yes, now you are laughing . . . embarrassed perhaps—that
makes me feel better, as you can imagine. And you are saying my
name or, rather, my nickname, as all priests do; and there's your
arm around my shoulders, and you've left me a package of food
you think I like. It is good to have your arm around my shoulders,
but I see, again, you are looking at your watch—that most common of our contemporary unknowingly demonic glances.

"Perhaps we won't have any further talks, you and I, for I see
you are able to dismiss them as anticipated madness or bad for me
to have, and, instead of encouraging me to live through my parables to their end, you want me to accept your affability as a substitute for love. After all, we are both in the great institution, living
our own stories out. Yes, you want to speak. I haven't let you talk
since you've come. No, I see. Perhaps it's enough for me that you
are somewhere here, that you come at all. There is no need for
you to get up, come to me and softly kiss me on the lips. My
brother, that would be—plagiarism." *

---

* Alyosha got up, went to him and softly kissed him on the lips.
"That's plagiarism," cried Ivan, highly delighted. "You stole that from
my poem. Thank you though." From "The Grand Inquisitor," *The Brothers
Karamazov.*

STRUCTURES OF INHUMANITY

I

AT THE PRESENT MOMENT witchcraft and Satanism are enjoying a mild popularity in the United States. It seems to me that these are simply faddish archaisms, and as such they will not concern me here. What I do want to consider is the demonic as a quality in the world of our contemporary experience. For this purpose I will use the term "demonic" in a very precise way, to refer to any transhuman powerfulness that is experienced as negating human life and human values. We should note the two elements in this definition.

On the one hand, I shall use the term "demonic" to designate what is encountered as a transhuman powerfulness. The essence of the demonic is power over the human situation, power to change, to control, to have disposal over the existence of people. But the demonic is not just any kind of powerfulness. It refers to such powerfulness as seems to come from *beyond all human agency.* We are familiar enough with the force that one person can wield over another person, that one group of people can bring to bear on another. We know only too well the degradation, the oppression, the exploitation and the cruelty to which people have subjected one another in every age of human history, and not least in our own day. So far as power seems to emanate from a recognizably human agent, we are not involved with what I am calling the demonic. Demonic powerfulness is experienced as surpassing the whole horizon of human activity. It releases a destruction or it opens up a magnitude, or it cuts through to a depth, or it involves a finality that no individual or corporate human agency could possibly attain.

116

In the traditional representations of the demonic in the West, we find that it is shown as operating in either of two ways: Sometimes it crushes and violates with overwhelming force, and, as such, may be associated with events of disease or insanity, famine or flood. In this mode the demonic is represented as a giant or a dragon, full of brutally destructive violence. At other times the demonic is experienced as securing its mastery over human beings, not by crude force, but by subtle insinuation, by playing on the weaknesses and perverse wishes of the human mind and thus seducing people to give themselves over into its power. In this mode the demonic is represented as a wily serpent taking on the appearance of a lovely woman or handsome man, manipulating and enslaving the human ego by means of enticing forms. In either mode, however, as terrifying or as seductive, the demonic signifies a powerfulness from beyond the human arena that ruthlessly dominates the lives of people.

Powerfulness, then, is one of its features. Its other feature is destruction of human life and human values. That is, the demonic, as I am using the term, belongs to a dual way of experiencing the world. It designates an agency that executes its powerfulness in an inhuman or anti-human way, in an evil way.

This awareness of duality developed in the West out of the Christian frame of reference, and is not found in many other traditions. In ancient China, for instance, transhuman powerfulness was identified especially with the power of wind and of water, and was commonly represented by the dragon. This powerfulness had no special association with destructive or anti-human activity. It could shatter, but it could also nourish and bless human life. It did not function at all within a duality-structured experience. Similarly in the mythology of Greece the *daemon* was an inferior divinity, sometimes an individual person's protective guardian and at other times the source of ill fortune.

By contrast, the Christian perspective has always been characterized by duality. For it trains people to see Jesus Christ in a theandric way, as the God-man in whom God's will and power are actualized for humanity. Approached in this manner, Jesus Christ stands forth in extreme opposition to destructive and anti-human powerfulness. In him God does not dazzle or overwhelm or intimidate, does not compel or degrade or exploit. In him God's powerfulness appears as serving and nourishing rather than as dominating. There is a striking saying to this effect in the Gospel of Luke

(22:25). The disciples began arguing about which of them would be the greatest and Jesus said to them: "In the world kings lord it over their subjects, and those in authority are called their country's 'Benefactors.' It shall not be so with you. On the contrary, the highest among you must conduct himself like the youngest, the chief of you like a servant. For who is greater—the one who sits at the table or the servant who waits on him? Surely the one who sits at the table. Yet here I am among you like a servant."

The contrast here between two kinds of powerfulness—one that dominates and the other that serves and nourishes—characterizes the whole Christian perspective. This duality came to structure the experience of many peoples in the West, who therefore developed a sense that a certain kind of powerfulness always exercised itself in an evil and destructive way, in opposition to the will and way of God. To this the word "demonic" came to refer.

Yet not all evil is demonic, not all represents the action of transhuman forces. Alongside of demonic evil stands human moral evil, the evil that is understandable within human terms—the wrong decision, the selfish goal, the hardhearted response. The demonic designates the destruction of human life and values that cannot be attributed to the moral self-conscious decisions of human beings. It is a term required by those occasions when people find themselves victimized by transhuman energies and structures.

Such is the meaning of "demonic" as I will use the term. I have stressed the experiential element, because I have no interest here in the demonic as a postulate for self-conscious explaining. It is certainly the case that many peoples have appealed to Satan or to devils in order to provide an explanatory cause for diseases or insanity. With this I have no concern. As I look at contemporary experience, it is not the demonic as a deliberately formulated explanation, but the demonic as a quality of destructive powerfulness encountered in the world that I wish to investigate.

II

It is an obvious law of nature that life feeds on life. All organisms need nourishment and have to derive it from other organisms. From this perspective, diseases in the human body are perfectly natural phenomena. They involve certain organisms supporting themselves within the body in such a way that the balance of one or another biochemical operation is upset and the bodily functions are impaired. Normally the body maintains life by its own natural vigor and adaptability. The presence of disease marks a debility in the body. The body fails to have enough vigor to nourish these other organisms while sustaining its own life, or enough adaptability to control and limit their presence. If we think of the organic realm as a network of mutual nourishment, then disease is a perfectly natural event, in essence no more abnormal than any ordinary meal which we enjoy.

It is an extraordinary thing that most people in the United States today do not look upon disease as a natural phenomenon—that is, as an instance of an operation that belongs naturally and universally to all life. On the contrary, as people imagine a disease, they tend to experience it as terrifyingly *abnormal*. In fact, in all popular accounts of disease *abnormality* is always the dominant theme: Disease represents, not a life-affirming process, but something life-negating, something disordered, destructive and anti-natural. If workers in the medical professions do not always share this viewpoint, they nevertheless depend on it and encourage it in their quest for Government funding and social power.

I wish to call attention particularly to three features of the prevailing sense of disease. First of all, disease is commonly thought of as an event of destructive power. There appears in the body some kind of harmful energy, some organic dynamism whose essential mark is to upset and destroy our life-processes. We commonly think of a disease taking over some part of our body, as if it had an energy of its own and by that energy could master one of our organs or tissues, negating the life that is in them. We often think of diseases as capable of spreading, or being characterized by a kind of drive to extend their destructive possession of our bodies.

What we are dealing with here is an experience patterned by duality. Contrary to all the testimony of science, disease tends to be pictured as a kind of anti-natural, anti-life energy. That is, cancer is taken as the paradigm of what disease really is, a spreading, devouring, life-destroying form of vital energy.

The opposition between the scientific understanding of disease and this folk-view is a matter of some importance. The scientific interpretation is not concerned with how a sickness may be experienced by a patient, but only with its symptoms, aetiology and effective cure, with how it appears to microscopic analysis and explanatory categories. Therefore it is exactly what the scientific approach disregards that the popular view takes as its central datum:

the characteristics of a disease for the patient who actually endures it. And from that perspective diseases do seem to drain away our energies, to impose an ordeal of pain, and to make us feel as if we were being ravaged by some destructive energy. In other words, while the duality notion, which opposes disease-energy to life-energy, makes little sense from the perspective of biological explanation, it does articulate a crucial element in the actual experience of sickness that the scientific view must in principle disregard.

Destructive powerfulness is one feature in the contemporary folk-view of disease. There is a second feature for which scientific studies have been chiefly responsible. This is the notion that disease comes into the body from outside. "Germs" or "bacteria" or "viruses" become the vehicles which carry this destructive energy into the human system. The whole idea of "infection," in fact, reinforces the view that a disease is somehow an outside energy that invades some part of the body and works dynamically to gain control of it.

For the popular viewpoint this coming-from-beyond-the-body does not express simply a matter of physical place. It carries the meaning of that which is alien, of that which belongs to a very different and incompatible biological framework. Disease does not come into the body from "outside" in just a spatial sense, but also in the sense of coming from *beyond*, from another realm and order, from outside that whole fabric of nourishment and life-support systems in which the body is favorably embedded. In other words, in this sense of "outside" there reappears that duality notion which sets the evil energy of disease in fundamental opposition to the good energy of life.

What emerges from this analysis is the way in which the popular notion of disease fulfills the characteristics of what I am calling the demonic. Illness is a matter of some quite alien powerfulness penetrating into our body and there exercising its energies with purely destructive effects.

There is, finally, a third feature of the contemporary situation which confirms this analysis in a curious way. Here I have in mind the striking but prevalent feeling of vulnerability before disease. Today it is not common for people to rely on the natural power of their bodies to preserve them against disease. They act as if their health were in a fragile and impotent state and unable to endure the least infection—that is, as if the demonic powerfulness of disease surpassed any defensive energy that their own bodies could naturally bring into play.

What people do, then, is to prop up the uncertain ability of their bodies with artificial supports, with vitamins, pills, drugs, and inoculations. They do this all the time, even when they are supposed to be healthy. When a sickness does appear, they do not dare to let it run its course while they depend on the body's own resources to overcome it. They seem convinced that the body has no adequate resources. Medicines or injections or surgical operations are necessary. So transhumanly powerful are diseases believed to be that we can "fight and overcome them," as the physicians like to say, only if we put into our bodies some equally transhuman counteractant. In our day there is something definitely obscure and occult about medicines. The fact that we are now quite prepared for them to produce dangerous side effects shows how conditioned we have become to the demonic character of the entire situation. In my view the fact that people show extraordinary pessimism about their own human resources in the face of sickness represents the most important sign that in this area they feel themselves subject to a demonic kind of powerfulness.

The patterns of experience which we find associated with disease are also in evidence in many other areas of contemporary life. Consider the way in which people have come to picture the character of war. There was a day when war was accepted as a normal instrument of national policy. It was conducted by men and controlled by men. It called forth the profoundly human virtues of courage and honor, and it was pursued for the sake of genuinely human values. In view of the overwhelming power of present-day military weapons such an attitude seems incredibly remote. Modern weapons produce such massive and thoroughgoing destruction that their use cannot in any way be justified in terms of the advancement of human goals or the enrichment of human life. They are too dreadful to be agents of proper human activity at all. It is therefore widely believed that anyone who would deliberately undertake massive war must in some way be insane. That he must have lost his human ways and fallen under the spell of the same destructive forces that he releases. War appears as the intrusion of some kind of transhuman and anti-human monstrosity into the human scene.

As something transhuman, it obviously cannot be dealt with by means of humane and rational measures. The impulse to war on the part of any nation is not really something that can be gathered into reasoned discussion. Just as in the case of disease, the only reliable counteractant to the threat of war is the use of instruments of equally massive power. Demonic powerfulness can be contained and turned aside only by equally monstrous power. Therefore, there can only be one reliable defense against war and that is the power of war itself.

It is rather eerie to watch how in the United States this demonic sense of war underlies the rhetoric of the Government's military policy. Since no sane nation would undertake war today, a sane country such as ours (so the reasoning goes) could only maintain its military establishment for the purpose of dealing with the barbaric insanity *of other peoples*. Hence in the United States—one of the most militaristic of all states and the supplier of militarism to countries all over the world—the military is called the *Defense* Department. This is not just pious and deceptive hypocrisy, a gloss behind which all kinds of aggression can be conducted. This name echoes the conviction that war is a transhuman demonism, which decent people only undertake in order to protect themselves against war itself, in order to provide shelter for the weak and fragile humanity of ordinary life.

At the other end of the scale from international conflict, consider how people tend to picture the hazards which may threaten their own individual lives. If the gas furnace explodes, if the car goes out of control, if the airplane crashes, these incidents are called "accidents." This term is much less innocent than it sounds, for it not only carries the meaning that such disasters do not result from any deliberate human doing (that is, they stand outside the range of human purpose) but the term also means that they belong to no order of purpose at any level of reality. Neither the intentions of some God nor the movements of some positive destiny are available to set these incidents in a context which gives them meaning. At every level they are accidents, irrational and absurd and detached from all significant purpose. That is to say, in these disasters people find themselves in touch with a totally disordered powerfulness that stands wholly outside the human order and in that sense is essentially demonic.

Even within the strictly human sphere incidents can trigger the contemporary sense of the demonic in diminished ways. Think of the ordeal of trying to cope with a bureaucratic process on which you depend in some way, but which suddenly fails to deal with you. For instance, perhaps the welfare check does not arrive. You go through the usual procedures in such a case, but they do not bring results. So you stand in line. You talk to an official. You are sent somewhere else. You sit in a crowded office. You finally talk to another official. You are told to come back the next day. You come back and are sent somewhere else. The devastating thing in such experiences is the discovery of the implacable nonhumanity within what appears to be a perfectly human process. The reason for this is obvious. In a bureaucratic system each worker is responsible only for executing a step *within the process*, and his or her attention is allowed to focus only on the process as such. As for the people that the process is supposed to serve and benefit, responsibility for them lies with no individual worker but only with the process itself as a whole. In fact, that is how the process is defined and justified in the first place: people are not served by responsible individuals but by the whole organization. If, in your case, the system fails, there is no one to take responsibility for you. Each functionary whom you visit will check only on that segment of the process that rests with him. However, because the total process is so complicated and the errors within it can be so subtle, so arbitrary and so unexpected—a confusion of names here, a slight mistake on the IBM card there, a faulty instruction somewhere else—it is extremely unlikely that you will ever find the right worker to ferret out the source of your difficulty.

In this kind of experience there is no outburst of obvious violence. One meets, instead, an exasperating absence of any rational or humane address to one's problem. The process empties one of any human reality, and the feeling of being crushed by a subtly inhuman and inflexible powerfulness can be severely intense. For people who are prone to experience the demonic in the world, the same sense of helpless victimization will easily come into play here.

This survey of various areas of contemporary experience—disease, war, accidents, and bureaucracy—indicates the presence of a belief in a demonic powerfulness, a powerfulness too great to be controlled by human resources and essentially destructive of human life and values. At present this belief is in a very primitive stage. It has little self-consciousness. It has no mythology associated with it. Cancer and war are the effects of a powerfulness that has no name and no form. Rationally we have to argue that for every activity there must be an agent. Yet in these experiences no effort is made to identify the agents which are working through this destructiveness. Life is felt to be threatened simply by strange forces that lurk beyond the circle of familiar existence, waiting to break in.

To associate this awareness with the old beliefs in a personal devil and in demons that have horns, tail and cloven feet after the fashion of the satyrs in Roman mythology is a profound confusion. For the people of earlier times were able to identify destructive powers with the grotesque ferocity of animal vitality. Satan was a monstrous dragon. St. Anthony was attacked in the desert by various wild and savage beasts that howled and brayed and sniffled, and attacked him with their horns and paws and teeth. A higher level of sophistication in the ancient world found its supreme experience of destructive powerfulness in terms of a deliberately malicious will. Then Satan was represented as a fallen angel.

For people today neither of these forms has much relevance. In the machine world of modern mass society, there is simply no encounter with powerful animal vitality, and the human will even of the most powerful leaders seems lost in the movement of vast forces beyond calculation. What is a mere dragon compared to the hydrogen bomb? How can a malicious will be taken with final seriousness in the face of the nightmare of overpopulation, where the most precious of all values—life itself—turns out to be, by its very vigor, a source of terribly inhuman destruction? For our age the demonic does not—and cannot—wear these old forms, but appears rather as a formless and impersonal dynamism that seizes upon us unexpectedly in the cancer cell, in the auto accident, in the cascade of napalm bombs, or more subtly in the impersonality of bureaucratic systems on which we depend.

With this sense of the demonic now in our midst, I find it no accident that newspapers and television programs offer us pictures of the mangled human body with almost liturgical regularity. To view a child in Vietnam burned with napalm or a bloodied corpse twisted inside a wrecked automobile is not to see simply a remote and unlikely oddity. For many people these pictures help body forth their own sense of the essential human condition, of mankind caught under the impact of a destructive powerfulness which is totally anti-human and before which the human form is pathetically impotent.

We should note one final aspect of this contemporary awareness of the demonic. It profoundly colors people's attitude toward final things, toward the largest and farthest horizons to which their minds can reach. In theology this is called "eschatology." What appears often today is the belief that if we extend our gaze beyond the human sphere we will find no meaning, no value and no life. We will find only the kingdom of the demonic. In other words death as the violation and extermination of life becomes the sign of all final realities. The human venture is a mere bubble in a chaos of blank and pointless power, and eschatology is a thoroughly negative arena. A passage in Thomas Wolfe's novel, *You Can't Go Home Again*, expresses this sense of ultimate things.

> There came to him here an image of man's whole life upon the earth. It seemed to him that all man's life was like a tiny spurt of flame that blazed out briefly in an illimitable and terrifying darkness, and that all man's grandeur, tragic dignity, his heroic glory came from the brevity and smallness of this flame. He knew his life was little and would be extinguished, and that only darkness was immense and everlasting. And he knew that he would die with defiance on his lips, and that the shout of his denial would ring with the last pulsing of his heart into the maw of all-engulfing night.

Many people today have such a sense of the demonic as ruling reality that in honesty they can only look upon ultimate things with this kind of despair.

III

Let me now turn to the question of how people cope with this sense of the demonic, how they actually gather this into their lives and let it shape their behavior. We must recognize that the entire cultural tradition which we carry at present stands totally opposed to this experience. It denies the existence of anything like the demonic. Let me briefly characterize this tradition, so that we can appreciate how threatening everyone finds the new awareness of the demonic.

The tradition which has long prevailed can be summed up in one principle: the world is favorable toward our humanity. Are we human beings creatures of reason? Then the world is rational. It is so constituted that its nature is in harmony with our subjective reasoning, and it actually makes itself available for our reasoning. If something is not rational, if in its essence and action it cannot be understood and cannot be enveloped in some context that explains it, then that thing does not exist, and anyone who believes that it does exist is simply the victim of superstition.

Are we human beings creatures of creative projects? Is making and fabricating the nerve of our humanity? Then the world is indeed receptive of our projects. It waits to be worked upon with our creative energies and to be gathered into our human projects. As the young Karl Marx insisted, nature is there to be humanized by our labor. The raw materials of the earth, the soil, the plants, the animals, the planets and stars exist for no other purpose than to serve the creative projects of the human race. But what about the other viewpoint? What about, say, the American Indians who refused to use the land because they believed that it belonged to the plants and the buffalo? By such an attitude they showed themselves to be subhuman and unworthy of life, or at least unworthy of being related to the land. But perhaps natural resources are limited. Perhaps the world prohibits the pursuit of some projects that are valuable and important for human life. Not at all. That is irresponsible defeatism. Nature is made for our human projects, and if one area of nature were to fail us, then human ingenuity will learn how to tap the resources in another area.

Are we human beings creatures of love? Is our highest humanity found in the service and affection and honor with which we can relate to one another? If that is so, then according to this tradition human beings are made to love and to be loved by one another. Is there an innate destructiveness and aggression in human beings, so that in taking on the attitude of love and in thus putting ourselves at the disposal of other people, we only pose an irresistible temptation to them to manipulate and exploit us? What a dreadful notion. Is there an innate fear within human beings, so that the closeness and oppressive claims of love always seem an intolerable threat? Preposterous. Since to be human is to love, then human nature as we actually find it must be made for loving and for being loved.

Such are three versions of the tradition that has long pervaded our culture. It is the tradition of humanism, which believes that the world around us favors and supports our human aspirations.

The experience of the demonic, as of an essentially and implacably anti-human powerfulness in the world, stands in opposition to this humanism. The tension between these two perspectives deeply affects the various ways by which people today cope with their experience of the demonic. Let me distinguish three such ways.

1. The first way might be called the state of dissociation. Most people simply live with these two viewpoints co-existing in their minds. There is the educated part of their consciousness, pervaded by humanistic triumphalism and full of bold confidence about the world and its support of all our human values. But alongside this they also carry an awareness of cosmic evil, of enormities in the world before which all human values are as nothing. Many people vacillate between these two states of mind, perpetually torn by this contradiction.

2. A second way might be called the attitude of submission. A few individuals refuse to exist in this schizoid condition. For them the humanistic tradition seems like a lie, a deception that has left them completely unprepared for the terrible demonic forces which they find threatening their lives. In anger they want to sweep away the lie of humanism. They want truth, and truth requires them to become the agents of, and the witnesses to, the demonic powerfulness which they find ruling existence.

In his novel *Dr. Faustus*, Thomas Mann gives an extraordinary portrayal of this nihilistic passion. For Leverkühn, the hero, life to its very core is absurd and chaotic. Therefore he is in violent reaction against the prevailing humanistic belief that the world has order and meaning. Beethoven, he is convinced, was mistaken. Therefore he undertakes his plan to compose a piece of music that would take back and "unwrite" Beethoven's 9th Symphony, that greatest of all musical celebrations to the harmony between man and the world. This monument to prevailing humanism is false, he believes, and must be revoked.

3. There is also a third attitude, which I would call the way of courage. Here, people move beyond humanism altogether. They do not hold onto it in a schizoid fashion, nor do they violently attack it and shatter it in submission to destructiveness. Instead, they start by accepting the demonic character of reality fully and, living primarily out of courage, work to resist the demonic and to maintain a sphere of human value for as long and as well as possible, without any illusions about—or even reliance on—the world. As one who articulates this attitude we think immediately of Albert Camus. Yet it is instructive to realize that the old Norse culture shaped all human life in terms of the necessity of courage. Judging by the Icelandic Eddas, these people had a pessimistic eschatology. While the present order of existence was, they believed, maintained by the gods, a great dragon lay encircling the

earth. According to the prophecies, the day would come when that
dragon would rise, would destroy the gods, and would engulf the
earth in sea. All things godly and human would then vanish away.
The prophecies of the ultimate power of the demonic also dis-
closed that this final convulsion would begin on the day when the
great wolf, now prowling near the gods, would attack and kill the
god Odin. Therefore, in order to preserve the order of the world
for as long as possible, it became necessary to restrain this wolf.
The dwarves were called in to make an unbreakable leash, and this
they did, fashioning a thin silklike band from the roots of a
mountain, the breath of a fish, and the sound of a snowflake. But
the wolf, ever suspicious, would not let this leash be tied around
his neck unless one of the gods placed his hand within the wolf's
mouth as a pledge. The god Thor offered his hand. The leash was
tied around the wolf's neck, and it held him so that he could not
break it. That is to say, the world order was preserved for a while
longer. But this was secured only at a cost, for the god Thor lost
his hand.

These Norse stories reflect a way of life which has no trace of
triumphal humanism and which seeks to maintain human values
in a world where the demonic is ultimate, where the last word can
only be defeat and disaster. In that situation one lives by courage
and by sacrifice. One knows that the order and stability of daily
life are fragile and temporary, and that in the struggle to preserve
them against destruction, sacrifices such as Thor's are an accepted
necessity. By contrast with this Norse attitude, it is sobering to
recognize how little courage is fostered in the upbringing of children in this country. Since people here are not trained in courage,
we can appreciate how helpless and terrified they must feel when
they become aware of the world as a demonic realm.

IV

Let me consider this contemporary experience of the demonic from
a Christian point of view—that is, in the light of the Biblical wit-
ness to Jesus Christ. In recent centuries Christianity has been
strongly affected by the prevailing humanism, with the result that
Christian theology has tended to ignore the demonic completely
and to take *human* wrongdoing as the primary form of evil. It has
claimed that the world is good, nature is good, and that the only
blot upon God's magnificent creation is the sinful human will. It

therefore has looked to Jesus to purify the human spirit of its
wrong choices and perverse desires, confident that once the mind
and heart of humanity were cleansed of sin, all would be perfect.

It is rather a shock to discover how far such a viewpoint is from
the entire Biblical perspective. For the Bible does not have a primarily moral understanding of the human situation, as if people's
lives were decisively shaped by the daily choices which they make.
Instead it understands the present human condition as a drastic
loss of all genuine moral life. It views sin religiously and not
morally. We can appreciate this if we distinguish two aspects in the
Biblical account of sin. On the one hand, sin constitutes a repudiation of the Lordship of God by humanity. In their existence people
refuse to acknowledge God as the basis of their life, as the origin
of their good and as the goal of their striving. But this repudiation
of God does not mean that they take God's place and themselves
rule the universe in his stead. The world is full of agencies and
dynamisms that completely transcend the reach of human reason
and the control of human power. According to the Bible, what is
actually entailed in the repudiation of God is a submission to these
other enormities. They are not gods, only beings created by God,
but they impose themselves upon people as if they were gods, as if
by their power they were the lords and disposers of human life. In
the Bible these are occasionally identified with Satan and the demonic. They may be enormities of nature or of society. They may
be uncanny occult impulses from beneath the earth or heavenly
forces that rule the stars. In any case sin is that repudiation of God
which subjects humanity to the control of these forces. And their
rule is necessarily destructive. This is because of the Biblical conviction that life depends essentially and universally upon a right
relationship to God. When humanity cuts itself off from that relationship, it becomes subject to forces and enormities that can only
bring destruction.

Thus we can understand why, from this Biblical perspective, sin
is not merely a series of wrong moral choices, but is a religious
event. When people turn from God and move into the control of
destructive enormities, they fall into a dreadful servitude. They
lose touch with the only ground for their effective freedom. Their
existence is enveloped by intimidating powers and by the destructive finality of death. Every moment of life thus becomes entram-
meled with the threat of the demonic. Free choice—the authentic
choice which grows out of the absence of fear and out of assurance

in the ground of one's own honor and vitality—such free choice completely vanishes from the human scene. No moral freedom is possible because, having lost touch with God, the entire structure of human existence finds itself victimized by demonic enormities.

From this Biblical perspective, then, it is simply not the case that the human mind and will are the only sources of evil. In the event of sin, humanity discovers a disorder in the cosmos far beyond its own horizons. It discovers magnitudes in the world that also seem to repudiate the Lordship of God. It discovers the demonic. In the Old Testament the overwhelming imagery for the demonic world, where life is cut off from God, is impotence, sickness and sterility. Everything is in a state of dissolution. There is much violence, but because the agents of this violence are not rooted in God—that is, in authentic reality—their apparent strength is a delusion which can exist only for a time. The demonic forces that assert their own glory instead of the glory of their creator—and the sinful person who, because he is cut off from God, must order his life to these demonisms—may flourish and display their vigor for a time. But their strength does not spring from reality itself; instead, it is artificial and abnormal. The Old Testament therefore often identifies this demonic and sinful activity with magic and whoredom. For these designate actions that seem to be full of strength, but in fact are hollow and barren and essentially vain. The Old Testament actualizes the cosmic dimensions of sin by developing a whole geography for the world into which sin moves people. Sinners find themselves inhabiting a desertland, full of fiery heat and severe winds, where their thirst for refreshment is always unappeased. They have no road and no goal, and therefore soon become lost. For how can there be any real direction of their existence in a land the essence of which is confusion and disorder and trackless waste? This geography is a metaphor for the world of dreadful sterility and victimization in which people who have become cut off from God eventually find themselves.

The New Testament is not so picturesque in its language, but is equally emphatic. As revealed in Jesus Christ, God stands forth as one who has nothing to do with absolute power, with a power that can produce square circles, or smash kingdoms or dissolve a universe. As encountered in Jesus Christ, God's power is that which nourishes and orders, which heals and rectifies. In Jesus Christ, God does not assert himself over against the world at the expense of the world, but affirms and reconciles the world to himself at the expense of his son. By comparison with Jesus Christ, most of the powers which people worship as God are intimidating and degrading, are in fact demonic. For the New Testament, as for the Old Testament, sin means bondage to destructive powers—above all to the decimating power of death. Even sin itself, according to Paul, is a power which masters and controls us and over which we have no control. "I am a slave of sin," Paul writes. . . . "It is no longer I who performs these actions but sin that lodges in me." (Rom. 7:14, 17)

We thus find in the Bible two important themes. First of all, the condition of sin is really a condition of terrible victimization. There is no trace of humanism there, no belief that the world is favorable to present human values. On the contrary, people find themselves subjected to inhuman powers from which they cannot escape—powers in nature, powers in society, powers beyond the horizon of present experience. Secondly, this whole realm of inhuman power and victimization is cut off from God and therefore, in spite of its appearance, is really impotent and sterile. It is a dissolving and debilitating powerfulness. It has no rootage in authentic and effective vitality. In this realm a destructive power may thrive for a time, but then it disintegrates; it becomes a specious pretense. Throughout Christianity, Jesus Christ is seen as exposing the pretense of all demonic powerfulness, including the apparent powerfulness of death, and as doing this because of the way his existence was rooted in the power of God.

I have been speaking in a rather abstract way. Let me point out the crucial role of the demonic in the work of Christian service. Humanism has taught us to expect that service to our needy neighbors, to suffering children, to enslaved prisoners, is bound to be successful. Suffering and despair will be eliminated by human caring. This is obviously false: the children continue to cry, the prisoners continue to grow weaker, the poor continue to die. At this point the humanist flees. Taught to relate to suffering for the sake of removing it, he is shattered when he discovers that his service can no longer help. When the patient's death is inevitable, the physician disappears and leaves him to the nurse. When the reform of welfare fails, the social activist turns away to another and more manageable project. In other words, humanism is not prepared for the demonic which confronts us in our suffering neighbors. Our age is full of the wreckage of humanistic projects that wilted before the demonic.

Anyone who has ever dealt seriously with human destitution, who has served in hospitals or in prisons or in impoverished villages, knows perfectly well that the most severe problem is not the hardness of human hearts but the intransigent and obscure forces that manipulate circumstances, intimidate leaders and frustrate service. To go out and serve the needy without being able to face up to the terrible powerfulness of the demonic is folly.

In this connection I would remind you that two very different approaches to the demonic are presented in the Gospel accounts about Jesus. There is one way of exorcism, where demonic powerfulness is driven away and people are liberated from bondage to disease or insanity. But this way is not given great attention. It does not carry any crucial value. In fact the New Testament makes absolutely clear that no one is going to exorcise the demonic out of this world. On the contrary, demonic inhumanity will increase. The present power and pervasiveness of demonic forces in the world is too extensive to imagine that they will be removed by exorcism.

The other approach is the way of the cross. Jesus calls upon people to take up his cross—that is, in some sense to enter into the arena of demonic suffering rather than to flee from it. This is the approach that receives primary emphasis in the New Testament. But what is this approach? What does it mean to take up Jesus' cross and to let oneself be attacked by inhuman dreadfulness?

The fundamental issue at stake here is the mode in which we discover the Lordship of God as an actual fact. It is easy to mouth the creed about God being almighty, but in the face of the powers that seem to rule this world such a belief remains unreal. Where and how do we actually discover for ourselves, as the truth of our own existence and of the existence which we share with our fellow humans, that the Father of our Lord Jesus Christ is indeed the only authentic power in all reality?

The only place we really discover this is where we are being attacked by demonic forces. It is one thing for God to rule by removing these dreadful forces from the scene, in the manner of exorcism. It is another thing for him to vindicate his rule precisely when, and as, these ferocities are in full activity. But what does it mean to say that he "vindicates" his rule at the very moment that the demonic displays its power in full force? What does this vindication amount to? As I see it, this is one of the meanings of Jesus' death. For on the cross Jesus did not submit to the demonic —that is, did not act as if it, and not his Father, were the master of his destiny. He refused to fear, to defend himself, to imagine that this dreadful destructivity had any final power over him. In short, while on the cross Jesus was sustained in his human way, in his confidence in his Father and in his compassion and care for those around him. God vindicated his rule in Jesus, not by removing the powers of destruction and death from him, but by maintaining in Jesus that supremely human condition of trust and love even while these powers worked their fullest.

To be sure, our lives may suddenly be delivered from suffering by an unexpected drug, by a political revolution, by a change of circumstance. Such blessings are not to be disdained. But the deepest discovery of God as the lord of life will occur decisively only as he proves able to sustain in us the humane strengths of trust and love while the demonic is at work. That is how I would understand the significance of Jesus' command to take up his cross.

Yet an odd thing happens very often. We may be most unnerved, most severely tested, most profoundly assaulted by the enormity of the demonic when victimization is imposed, not on us, but on others whom we cherish. That is when we are most tempted to despair of God, to let anger or panic possess us, and then to turn away from those very persons who suffer in order to preserve our own sanity. To companion another who is dying without withdrawal, to continue working with the poor after all resources have failed, to maintain one's trusting and one's loving when the forces of demonic inhumanity seem to be in full control—as I see it, that is what it means to take up Jesus' cross. This is what it means to be with and to serve the neighbor, not with triumphal humanism, but in His name. This dimension of service, however, only begins when one is willing to endure the impact of demonic enormities.

Let me conclude with reference again to the Norse legends. Because defeat and disaster stood at the last horizon, courage was the indispensable condition for every moment of life. The Christian perspective does not share that ultimate pessimism. It does, however, see the taking on of demonic suffering as an essential part of the love of neighbor and of the knowledge of the power of God. Courage, then, becomes a primary form of Christian faith. The contemporary experience of the demonic points us to this need for extraordinary courage.

Ann B. Ulanov

THE PSYCHOLOGICAL REALITY
OF THE DEMONIC

THE SUBJECT of this essay is the psychological reality of the demonic: how the demonic shows itself to us in all the languages of the psyche, the language of consciousness and the unconscious, in relation to other people, relation to our world, and in our relation to God. To speak of the psychological reality of the demonic, we must first remind ourselves that the psyche has objective existence. The hardest thing to grasp about the unconscious is that it exists, and that it is unconscious. It is both there and not there; it is the "other side," so to speak, that which is darkness to our light, that which is unknown to what we call familiar, that which comes from the other side of our motives, from the other side of our virtues and the other side of our vices.

As we all know, in addition to our conscious, ego-centered point of view, there is a vast area in the psyche that is unconscious. As Jung made clear, consciousness itself arises out of the unconscious, gradually forming its own position. In spite of our ordinary everyday experience, in which we think of ourselves as a subject for whom others are the objects of our attention, for whom even the unconscious is an object of attention, the reverse is really the case. Our consciousness, our subjective state, is the object of some prior subject out of which it has slowly differentiated itself.

The objectivity of the psyche is particularly relevant to our interest in the demonic, because above all else the demonic presents itself to us as an "other," as that which challenges our subjective viewpoint, even breaks in upon it, confronting the light of our conscious discernment with its own dark presence. This leads to my first focus; namely, a description of the demonic.

134

I Demon and Daimon

This word has two principal meanings: that of the demonic and the daimonic. Each is a *numen*, a working of a higher power, a greater than human power. The daimonic calls to mind the *daimon* of Socrates, which inspires, guides, and confirms a source of value beyond human conventions. The daimon, in this understanding, is also seen as a helpful fate urging self-realization and realization of truth, as a bridge between the human and the divine, as that which drives us beyond our narrow limits, beyond the hedges of conventional points of view. In Latin, the daimonic is associated with the word "genius," from the verb "to generate" or "beget." Thus the daimon has been thought of as all those sources of vitality which assert, affirm, confirm, and augment human personality, as the energy that fights against apathy, boredom, rigidity, and even death.

The second meaning of the demonic denotes a destructive power, an evil spirit in the New Testament sense, that works moral destruction on human personality. The demonic in this negative sense may derange the spirit, violently possess a soul, throw a person out of himself, disturb his relations with the good and move him toward identification with Satanic evil itself.

Both the daimon and the demon confront us with an "other" who is an adversary. But "adversary" can also be taken in two ways—the adversary that can be transformed into one's advocate, and the adversary that transforms itself into an antagonist unalterably opposed to human concerns. To experience the demonic as advocate is to encounter something other than ourselves pleading for a wider perspective than a subjective, ego-centered point of view. Tillich described such a demonic force as "a unity of form-creating and form-destroying strength." [1] It is that vital force which breaks through our present form in order to reach a higher form, and not simply to disrupt or destroy us. The human personality as a bearer of form in its totality and in its unconditioned character is a principal object of demonic forces. But the demonic as advocate is a vital force which erupts through one's present coherence in order to enlarge it. The demonic often pleads for a wider view, a deeper perception, a more passionate relationship to something beyond the ego. How does this feel? How do we describe this? The best way, I think, is in terms of those few central personal experiences that happen to us in the course of our lives, when we feel summoned, addressed, faced, even faced down, called to move from the place where we are to some unknown other place. Such experience is filled with all the terrors, risks, and hazards of the unknown. We feel such a summons as a command, as an imperative of conscience that we dare not disregard.

Jung distinguishes between two kinds of conscience, the second of which touches on the two functions of the demonic as advocate and as antagonist. One level of conscience—what we customarily call the "superego"—is developed from the incorporation of standards of conduct taught to us as children by our parents, teachers, and social leaders. The second kind of conscience confronts us as "other," as a numenous imperative that operates as if it were autonomous and should be regarded as the voice of God. This second level of conscience seems to be an independent instinctive reaction of the psyche that appears whenever we stray from the path of conventional mores. This voice of conscience can be positive or negative, a demonic "other" serving as advocate or antagonist. As Jung writes:

> The moral reaction is the outcome of an autonomous dynamism, fittingly called man's daemon, genius, guardian angel, better self, heart, inner voice, the inner and higher man and so forth. Close behind these, beside the positive, "right" conscience, there stands the negative, "false" conscience called the devil, the seducer, the evil spirit.[2]

We can never know initially when this other, the adversary, will appear and face us, perhaps to direct us to a new kind of illumination or to extinguish altogether what little light we do possess. We do not know at the outset which way it will go. Positive or negative, however, the demonic is adversarial; it will challenge our moral life fully. We will be put to the test, the testing of our values and the meaning of our lives, and we can be sure that the outcome will have far-reaching influence on the rest of our lives.

The opposite of the demonic as advocate is not evil but rather a kind of boredom, of dullness—a safe life lived according to the rules, but a life that has nonetheless forfeited the passions of certainty. We all have our own versions of this safe narrowness that excludes things we do not want to dwell on for fear they will threaten a relationship, thoughts we do not want to remember for fear they will challenge a comfortable self-image. We all have actions we rush into, for fear of sitting still and letting something slowly evolve. And the only direction to take, I think, when the demonic as adversary appears on the scene, is to hold on, to wait, maintaining one's conscious position in the face of the other in order to see what may evolve out of the tension.

The second kind of adversary, the demonic as antagonist, is a little different. It confronts us not as blinding light or ecstatic passion, but comes in darkness, density, blackness, and seems to be malevolent, sinister, and fearsome. It seduces us to retire into sloth, into refusing to be all that we can be. We all know bits and pieces of this experience of the demonic also. Most of us sense a darkness in ourselves we prefer not to bring into the light, full of prowling memories, haunting inferiorities, secret flatteries and self-beguilings —all that we would rather forget or disown. We prefer not to see our lack of real interest in anything outside our own lives. We do not want to admit that we are loath to develop a current ambition because of the work involved. We prefer to hide a deep streak of kindness that we may possess, for fear of others' ridicule. This inner darkness, this density, contains all that we find cheap or tawdry, unclaimed or disowned in ourselves, all that we would prefer not to think of as our own. Jung describes these areas of darkness with the symbol of the shadow. It follows us everywhere, but we cannot face it. It comes up behind us, but we do not see it. It is darkness to our light, denseness to our lucidity, opaqueness to our clarity. But the shadow also gives us depth, perspective—three-dimensional perspective—and history as well, for it stretches behind us to where we have been.

One cannot help recalling that old Sunday afternoon radio program called "The Shadow." It was always introduced by a question and an answer: "What Evil lurks in the hearts of men? The Shadow knows." If you want to have a quick idea of what your own shadow is, think of someone, usually of your own sex, for whom you have instant and abiding dislike. If it is not a particular person, it will be a particular type. And think in your mind: "I hate So-and-So because . . ." and then complete the sentence, listing all the unattractive characteristics you can think of. Put the list away. Tomorrow take the list out again. To learn to live with your shadow is like learning to live with a roommate you really do not like—and facing the threat of having the mate for life! [3] But the shadow figure is in fact indeterminate. One never knows whether it will transform itself into advocate or antagonist. It can develop either way: toward the daimonic, the advocate, to try to find courage to create our unique being-in-the-world, or it can move toward the negative pole, as an antagonist leading us into a malevolent darkness that destroys meaning.

The demonic as antagonist points toward the Satanic, that which disrupts form simply for the sake of smashing it. The opposite poles of form-disruption and form-creation are held in tension in the demonic but fly apart in the Satanic; the disruptive pole spins off autonomously, living only for itself, as a part elevated to the place of the whole, without regard for the rest of the personality or for anyone else. Yet with all this destructive effect, the Satanic is still only symbolized.[4] Unlike the demonic, the Satanic does not have actual existence. The demonic exists as a tension of creative and disruptive forces within the psyche. The Satanic symbolizes only the negative side.

Jung's concept of the shadow makes a similar point. The shadow is a psychic complex that mediates between the ego and all the repressed material that is unconscious. At the heart of this complex lives an archetypal core that springs from a deeper non-personal, objective dimension of the psyche that never appears directly in consciousness. We know of this archetypal effect on the psyche. When confronted by a demonic shadow figure we never know whether it can be integrated by the ego, or whether it will pull the ego away from human reality into the impersonal archetypal depths of the psyche.

The following dream illustrates how a shadow figure may appear first as negative and then as positive. A man dreamt that he was being relentlessly hunted down by another man whom he had betrayed. As a result of the betrayal, the second man had been incarcerated, either in a prison or a mental home, for a long time. Now he was out and hunting for the dreamer. One definitely feels apprehension in this opening scene. But the dream shifts; the second scene takes place at night in the middle of Central Park in New York. The dreamer is surrounded by thugs who are certainly going to rob him, if not kill him. But just then the man whom the dreamer had betrayed in the first part of the dream steps out from the group of thugs and slips into the dreamer's pocket a wallet full of money and then somehow takes the thugs away. The dreamer is suddenly free. In other words, that which appears to be menacing and full of vengence may be seeking to find us and meet us, to enrich us instead of rob us, to save us instead of kill us.[5]

A shadow figure can also remain negative and lure us beyond the level of personal material to a level of archetypal evil that seems to be so impersonal and unalterably opposed to human consciousness that we can react only with horror. The following dream of a man illustrates this:

> I came to a large house for dinner. The dining room was dark. The only illuminated place was the head of the table where a fat, evil-looking man was about to carve the meat for dinner. I was the only guest. He took a long, sharp carving knife in his hand. He lifted the cover from the platter and there on the platter was a hideous, foreign, altogether alien creature in the act of attacking and killing a chicken. This "thing" and the chicken were put in the oven at exactly that moment of attack and cooked with the creeping monster on the chicken's back. As the fat man went to cut into the 'thing,' it moved and I realized it was not yet dead, but fully alive. I was filled with unspeakable horror.

This level of raw, rapacious, predatory power—of natural evil, we might say—had nonetheless to be eaten for dinner, thereby suggesting that in some way it must be integrated. We know from theological tradition that evil finally is a mystery, a darkness we cannot penetrate, a nonexistence that nevertheless makes its presence felt; one might say evil is the presence of absence. This leads me to a second focus.

II Concrete Forms of the Demonic

The demonic is not just a private inner experience; it shows itself to be an autonomous other that confronts us not only in our own depths, but also in our politics, in our society, in history, in all forms of collective human life. The demonic is a vivid example of the psyche as objective. For each of us individually, there is no escape from trying to see this other and come to terms with it. Failure to do so, failure to see the demonic other, whether as advocate or antagonist, is, I think, a common source of the negative transformation of the demonic in the direction of the Satanic. We avoid seeing the demonic in two principal ways. We either become possessed by it or try to repress it. Either has serious negative implications for us.

Possession by the demonic means that the conscious personality is invaded, captured and brought under the sway of the demonic element. Any natural part of the psyche can assume demonic form if it usurps the place of the whole. In psychological language this state of possession is frequently called "psychic inflation," indicating a point where the ego falls into a state of unconscious identity with some aspect of the unconscious and is puffed up out of all human proportion by the instinctive energy-drive of that impersonal unconscious force. The ego feels driven by a source of energy not its own. Riding on the crest of this wave of unconscious energy, the ego inflates to larger than life size; it may even burst through its proper limits, driven to some manic excess. Thus a person in such a manic state may go without rest or food, propelled into being "on" all the time, accelerated, flying high. One is intoxicated, skating along at a dizzying pace, fearing only the inevitable letdown at the end. In such a state of possession, one does not see the demonic elements that need to be faced and slowly assimilated. One identifies with them instead and falls under their spell. For example, I do not see my resentment; I become my resentment. I do not feel my euphoria; I am my euphoria. I am compelled to live whatever unconscious "other" has invaded my consciousness and express its dynamism with an intensity that seems almost nonhuman.

At a time like this, the unconscious may reveal the dangers of such an ego possession, a form of revelation that usually surpasses the conventional common-sense warning that one is riding for a fall. The dream I am about to describe draws on ancient religious imagery to suggest a grave danger concealed in a state of ego-inflation. One flirts with the possibility of making a pact with the devil. This is a trivial, almost charming dream, yet imbued with a menacing undertone. A young man dreamt:

> I was in the underground world of the devil. It was a fascinating world. Everyone got about on roller skates. There was only one problem. Occasionally there were gaps in the surface of the road, and when you struck a gap, you would fall. Your skates would hit the ground and get stuck. Before you could get back on your way, you would have to stop, put your skates back on and then put your feet back upon the road's surface. The devil appeared and offered to make a deal with me, to show me how to navigate the gaps so that I could skate smoothly.

The devil offers an easy way out. In return, though unstated, the dreamer will give something; namely, his soul. If the dreamer learns to navigate the gaps, his ability to skate along the surface of reality is completed, because it is only when he hits a gap that his feet touch the ground. The dream warns that his desire for superficial ease may close all the "gaps," and cost him his hold upon reality.

Possession by a demonic element can also manifest itself as a kind of frenzy, as if one is gnashing to pieces even what one loves and is, as a result, being gnashed to pieces oneself. One is seized by an excess of emotion and opinionating; one is given over to outrage, indignation, and protest that is so powerful in its dynamism that one is led to fancify and falsify the wrongs done against oneself in order to justify beyond any doubt the correctness of one's own position. One is possessed by the need to be right, to win, even though such an aim alienates the very person to whom one may be trying to bring one's feelings. This particular kind of frenzy often happens to women, especially in relation to some one person or value they cherish dearly. It is as if a woman were grabbed by something outside herself and driven to gnashing to bits that which she loves, spewing out words with faultless, relentless, destructive logic. The only trouble is that her premises are all wrong. A young woman who could not come to terms with shadow elements in her personality, even though they were positive elements, serves as an illustration of this sort of demonic frenzy. She could not accept the fact that the qualities she so envied and admired in other women were qualities she could herself develop as part of her own personality. The particular qualities she had the most difficulty claiming as her own were capacities for independent aggression and focused intelligence. By not claiming these capacities, she fell into unconscious identification with them. Hence, they possessed her; they filled her negatively. In relation to her husband, her aggression, which might have become a capacity for initiative and confident self-assertion, took a wild turn and spun off into its own orbit, independent of and without regard for her affection for him. Her capacity for focused intelligence fastened on all the wrong things; so that, for example, if they were having an argument, she could never let the argument end; always, just as it was petering down, she would become inflamed again, seized by another not necessarily relevant issue. Or, if her husband said, "I feel this" in a way that really touched her, she would focus on the wrong thing, a funny expression in his eyes, for example, and say right off, "Well, if you really felt that, then why do your eyes look so strange?" And they would be off again. She smashed the very person she was trying to reach, smashed the very affection she felt for him. She could not gain real access to it; this demonic other invaded and took her off in a whirlwind.

In all states of possession, two things happen: there is a failure to see the other and to relate to it, and there is an accompanying failure to see one's own position and relate to it. Where one's ego should be filled with personal reactions, aims, possibilities, plans, good and bad feelings, there is instead a vacancy. There is no personal standpoint to withstand and to intercept the invasion of unconscious elements. As the New Testament makes clear, to clean your house of one devil, and go off leaving it empty, invites seven devils to take up residence in the unoccupied space. Failure to hold one's own point of view with vigor leaves the ego helpless before the assault of the unconscious.

Failure to see the other also results in failure to reach and hold onto oneself. The demon of possession dispossesses the ego. The other whom we would not acknowledge moves in and takes all the available space for itself. Negative inflation is an example of this situation, where one is compulsively deflated, caught by negative elements that usurp the place of the ego. A woman who had strong feelings of inferiority illustrates this state of deflation. She could not consciously see or relate to her feelings of inferiority as other than herself; they inhabited her instead. To anyone who tried to reach out to her with a friendly gesture or a supportive word, she seemed to protest, "Don't shoot! Don't shoot!" Then the person would say, "But, look, I don't want to shoot. I haven't got any guns or knives or anything." But he would barely finish that sentence when she would say again, "No, don't shoot! Don't shoot!" This goes on for so long that one has no other alternative—one wants to *shoot* her! This raises the very difficult issue of contamination.

When we are possessed, we are not the only ones hurt; we also contaminate others. Theoretically this fact can be explained on the basis that the psyche is objective. What we do in relation to our own psychic experience affects others, whether we know them personally or not. For example, when primitive forces of the demonic appear in the unconscious and one disregards them, it is as if one is unconsciously drawn toward all others who do the same by the presence of similar symbolic imagery. All together form a mob. The person who is made leader of the mob is the weakest of the group—he or she that is least defended against the powerful onslaught of unconscious energy pressing for release. The leader is the one most easily possessed, most easily taken over, who most desperately needs a sense of power, because he lacks an ego of sufficient strength.

When we are invaded by the demonic, collectively or individually, we are compelled to act out its wishes, we lack what Freud calls in his wonderful phrase, the "procrastinating function of thought." We act in spite of ourselves, in spite of our values; we let loose into the collective atmosphere untamed, unhumanized emotions and power lusts that infect others with the same fever. We thirst for victory for our side. We thirst for revenge against our enemies. We degenerate to the level of an "us-them" mentality. An ardent peace-movement member said to me recently, "Even though the present Vietnam peace is not total, Nixon's peace is an improvement and it is infuriating that he should get credit, any credit! Once again he sneaks out from under. He should have to pay!" Hardly a peace-loving attitude! It is as if the other side of this man's conscious position is left in darkness, and looms out of him, perhaps even unknown to him, contaminating his conscious desires for peace, and infecting the people around him with his untamed hostility. Such unassimilated affects can compel compulsive behavior that kills or ruins lives. This has something to do with the phenomenon of war, which I want now to discuss in terms of the second way we fail to see the demonic, when we repress it.

In repressing a demonic element, we push it far away, down into the unconscious life, free to roam wherever it pleases, free to mix with anything else that dwells in the unconscious, becoming more and more undifferentiated, more and more mixed up with other emotions, seeping into emotions that are consciously at our disposal. So that, for example, if one has a genuine sweetness, it is as if something were starting to contaminate its fine quality; one's sweetness becomes cloying, maudlin, and mixed with ulterior motives. Moreover, as we know, any repressed content must find release. The handiest release is through projection. Thus what I fail to acknowledge in myself, I will somehow see on your face. The anger I will not claim in my own heart, I will accuse you of feeling, and if you did not feel it before I came into your company, you certainly will feel it by the time I leave, because I will be trying so earnestly to fix it up and cure it in you, rather than claim it in myself.

There is social significance to this issue of repression too. One factor in all phenomena of social oppression, such as war, preju-

dice, or persecution, is personal repression. Wherever there is social oppression, personal repression is at work. We all build up
burgeoning shadow sides that press more and more for release the
more we repress them. We then find ourselves maneuvering others
into the role of enemies upon whom we can vent our spleen and
against whom we can indulge in a vast catharsis of repressed unconscious material. In war, all the outlawed unconscious impulses
burst forth in triumphant vengeance. We let loose all those destructive impulses in the name and cause of victory for our side.
We now have as our "enemy" a collective scapegoat for our
shadow side; we now indulge to excess what heretofore we denied
as any part of ourselves—thieving, bestiality, criminality, murder.
It would be much better if we endured individual psychic conflict
between our ego values and demonic shadow elements and enjoyed
external peace with each other, rather than the other way around
where we fight our shadows by fighting our neighbors, on whom
we project the demonic element. If each of us wrestled with the
demonic within we would draw near to each other as fellow suf-
ferers, rather than drawing apart as enemies.

The repression of the other side has another effect as well; it is
fatiguing. Tremendous energy is needed to keep things out of consciousness and the great drain on one's energy is constant. One can
be slowly dragged underground into the ancient sin of sloth. Like
that funny animal that hangs by its toes from trees, sleeping
through life, we are turned quite upside down. Where consciousness should be, unconsciousness reigns. We fail to use what we
have; we fail to develop our own being, to assert our own person-
hood. We refuse to be what we have been summoned to be and as
a result all this unused psychic energy turns into sheer poison,
tending to dissociate the personality from reality. Even if we can
survive this in ourselves, we are bound to have a very negative
effect on others and on any effort another may be making to affirm,
assert, or increase himself, his relations, and the richness of his
world. Something comes from us that attacks the other's self-
confidence.

This state of repression can reach proportions that psychologists
call a schizoid state in which one is split apart from one's world
and from one's self. Kierkegaard describes the schizoid condition
as a "state of shut-upness," where the demonic element "lives in
dread of the good." [6] The good is the return to freedom, human
contact, salvation, cheerfulness. The state of "shut-upness" is in-

tense withdrawal, muteness, closure. Even if we chatter about hypochondriacal symptoms, we never say a word about the real problem. Even if we drone on tediously about weighty subject matter, we refuse to reveal what is really important. In an argument we may know instinctively that we are in the wrong and know with certainty that if we say, "Oh, I'm sorry, I'm wrong," that will end the dispute, but we will not say it. Instead, we talk and talk and talk; present reasons to justify our behavior and insist upon demonstrating where the other is to blame, or even, on occasion, where we are to blame. But we don't say the essential thing. It is as if we cannot say it. How many times has an argument come to the point where we think: "I surrender. I give up. I throw down my arms, I open my arms." But we do not say those words or embrace those feelings even when we know that that is the only essential thing to be said. This is a state of "shut-upness." We refuse; we hide. As Kierkegaard describes it, this is the state of the demonic that wills to be itself in terms of its own misery.[7] It wills to be itself in a fit of spite, to obtrude on the power which harbored its existence and to hold out against it through malice. It is a reckless splurge of masochism, revolting against the whole of existence, taking one's misery as proof against the goodness of existence. It is the "Yes, but . . ." syndrome. No matter what is suggested, we reply, "Yes, good idea, but . . ."

In each example I have given of the demonic and our failure to see it in its concrete forms of possession, manic defense, repression, projection, contamination, and shut-upness, the failure is always the same—we do not see the other. In each encounter with the demonic other, its nature is always indeterminate. We do not know if it will move toward the good or the evil, toward the daimon, the advocate that fights against us for a wider, deeper self, or toward the demon, the antagonist who pulls us toward the mysterious realm of evil, symbolized by the Satanic. Which direction this other takes, whether it will move toward a positive or negative transformation, depends a great deal on the reaction of consciousness. This leads me to my last point: dealing with the demonic in psychic terms.

III *Dealing with the Demonic*

To deal with the demonic raises the question of the place of consciousness. How consciousness reacts to the demonic other seems to be an essential determinant for the way in which the demonic is transformed. The danger of mass psychic epidemics, for example, arises in direct proportion to the lack of consciousness on the part of each individual. From a therapeutic standpoint, it is absolutely essential to build up a conscious point of view so that there is something to intercept and assimilate the contents breaking through from the unconscious. Shadow elements are not necessarily destructive in themselves. They may turn out to be advocates of the wider, deeper self, but initially they are always ambivalent. If we turn away from the demonic other we give it no channel for its positive transformation or integration into consciousness. If we try to see and to relate to the demonic other we have a chance to come to terms with it and not be destroyed by it.

The guiding attitude in dealing with the demonic, I think, is to respect it, in the simplest meanings of the word "respect": to see it, to observe it, to give it close attention, to regard it; not to become this other and fall into identification with it, nor to run away from it or repress it. We need really to see this other and that involves being aware of one's own reaction to the other. From our own responses we can get small but distinct signs of what kind of demonic element—advocate or adversary—we are up against. On the simplest level, for example, in the face of natural evil, one usually has an instinctive response of natural self-preservation.[8] Our instincts tell us "Flee, save yourself, get away!" Such warnings are sometimes given in dreams that are full of natural catastrophes—a tidal wave is coming, or fire has broken out everywhere and is unstoppable. When our instincts warn us to take cover and protect ourselves, they are telling us that this encounter is not something that can be reduced to a personal challenge. To pit our puny strength against the tidal wave? That is a wile of the devil to tempt us to think that with the devil's help we might possess the power to match a tidal wave. On another level, when we meet a demonic other, it pays to watch carefully how it reacts if we respond with the New Testament counsel to love our enemies. What does this other do with the libido and attention we give to it? Does it use this energy to transform itself into a more positive expression? Or does it just swallow and devour this energy and grow fat on it and ask for more? If that is the case, then we can be sure we are feeding a demon.

An example of a positive transformation, as a result of the ego's positive response, is the change that occurred in the image of a dog in a series of a man's dreams that were dreamt over many months. In the first dreams of the series, the dreamer, a middle-aged man, was threatened by giant dogs about to leap for his throat. In these dreams, the dreamer always ran away. Then there appeared a dream in which the dogs were leashed. Here the dreamer stood his ground, though with great fear. Then there appeared a series of dreams in which there was only one dog, tied to a tree. As we discussed, in therapy sessions, the meaning of the dog image and why it might want contact with the dreamer, the man's attitude toward the dogs grew more receptive. Even in his dreams the dreamer began to respond to the dog, at first waving from a distance. As the dreams recurred over a period of months, the dog gradually grew smaller until it was finally just a yapping pup. Then in the last dream of the series something startling happened: the dreamer walked up to the dog, still tied to the tree, dropped to his knees, and barked back! The dog underwent a remarkable metamorphosis in response to the transformation in the dreamer's attitude: it changed into a little boy.

If our efforts to respond to an unconscious image leads to no change on the other side, so that we seem to be pouring our energies into a bottomless hole, then we know we are up against a demon that will feed off us until there is nothing left to give. What do we do then? We starve it. We give nothing—no libido, no interest, no attention, no energy, no blood, no warmth, no life. We save all of that for the conscious side.

This refusal to be charitable to an antagonistic demon, in my opinion, accords with Jesus' words, "Resist not evil." Do not take it on in order to reform it or change it. We only get caught, contaminated, filled up with the very feelings we are trying to fight; we are consumed with resentment, power lust, and a utilitarian motive to do something. Evil is never cured by interfering action. To say this is not to advocate passive withdrawal or any kind of know-nothing, care-nothing attitude. Evil is only met by building up the good, and goodness cannot be approached from a utilitarian standpoint. One may well ask: "What is goodness good for?" And the answer: "Nothing. Goodness is good for nothing. Goodness is." [9]

Another conscious attitude that can fatally entangle us with the negative demonic is frivolous curiosity. We are fascinated by this dark demonic other; we want to poke at it simply to see what will happen. We lack sufficient regard for it. We indulge in an idle curiosity about what effect we can create by prodding respect for mystery, treating it like a little problem we can solve, reducing it to the level of personal challenge, as if all of life matched our own small proportions. We have to see the other, respect it for what it is, and sometimes *not* see it as well, not insisting on knowing all, but respectfully giving it wide berth.

The *Cloud of Unknowing* offers similar advice when we are caught by sin and the tempting devil. It counsels us to look past the sin, to look over the devil's shoulder.[10] That way we do not repress our awareness of the presence of a demonic element, but neither do we fall into toe-to-toe combat with it, a battle that would sap the very energy we need to choose not to sin. We are to look past it, over its shoulder, to the figure of Christ, to the good. If that fails, then we simply surrender—our sin, our self, our every-thing—to the good. This leads to my final remarks about dealing with the demonic, looking to the place of consciousness.

Throughout this essay I have emphasized how important con-sciousness is, how we must react to the demonic element to keep it from usurping the place of our ego, and how the nature of our reaction seems to affect the transformation of the demonic ele-ment into advocate or adversary. We must be careful, because consciousness itself can be possessed by the negative demonic, the antagonist. We can be inflated, carried away to manic proportions by the power of consciousness to understand, label, and catalogue human reality. The result then is a violation of the human per-son. Consciousness is an indispensable ingredient in the transforma-tion process of the demonic, but it is only an ingredient, and only by reaching this greater development of consciousness are we met by the rich paradox that completes it, the knowledge in full con-sciousness that there are times when we must surrender conscious-ness. In religious language, we must renounce it, give it up, give it over, lest it become the agent of demonism in the negative sense, inflated beyond its proper limits, boundless in its expectations to handle everything, to find a way so that all psychic life comes to be viewed only in terms of consciousness. Here psychology needs religious perspective and religious language to describe that mo-tion of the soul that such a relationship to consciousness requires. It is of the order of grace to move easily and unthinkingly between conscious and unconscious psychic dimensions without a categori-cal shifting of gears. This is the area of guileless simplicity that moves us to feel, in the company of St. Thomas, that all our work to be conscious, all our achievement of a differentiated personality, is so much straw in the face of the experience of the other. As

Kierkegaard puts it, "The only power which can compel shut-upness to speak is either a higher demon (for every devil has his turn to reign) or the good, which is absolutely able to be silent." [11] The demonic expects of us nothing less than an emulation of the simple being of the Divine, an imitation of its immutability insofar as our complex nature permits. Thus we simplify, we accept the negative, without condoning it; we permit evil, rather than acquiesce to it. We permit evil to turn into good, allow it to be a supporter of the good, and extension of it. And all of this complicated striving to become conscious is done in order to make us less complicated, to offer consciousness to what is beyond consciousness; and curiously, though we are conscious, to allow us not to identify with our consciousness. We have achieved the remarkable ability to be unconscious.

NOTES

1. Tillich, P., trans. N. A. Rasetzki, Part I; trans. Elsa L. Talmey, Parts II, III and IV, *The Interpretation of History* (New York: Scribner's, 1936), p. 81.

2. Jung, C. G., trans. R. F. C. Hull, *Civilization in Transition, Collected Works*, vol. 10 (New York: Pantheon, 1964), p. 447.

3. For additional discussion of this exercise, see Ulanov, A. B., "The Two Strangers," *Union Seminary Quarterly Review*, vol. XXVIII, no. 4, Summer, 1973, p. 280.

4. See Tillich, *op. cit.*, pp. 80–81.

5. For additional discussion of this dream, see Ulanov, A. B., *op. cit.*, p. 279. This and all other dreams cited in this essay are taken from my private practice as a psychotherapist.

6. Kierkegaard, S., *The Concept of Dread*, trans. Walter Lowrie (Princeton: Princeton University Press, 1957), pp. 110–111.

7. Kierkegaard, S., *The Sickness Unto Death*, trans. Walter Lowrie (New York: Doubleday, 1954), p. 207.

8. I am indebted here to the thinking of Marie Louise von Franz. See especially, *Shadow and Evil in the Interpretation of Fairy Tales*, Part II (Spring: Zurich, 1974).

9. See Murdoch, Iris, "On God and the Good," in Greene, M., ed., *The Anatomy of Knowledge* (Amherst: University of Massachusetts Press, 1969), p. 254, where she writes: "The Good has nothing to do with purpose, indeed it excludes the idea of purpose. 'All is vanity' is the beginning and the end of ethics. The only genuine way to be good is to be good 'for nothing' in the midst of a scene where every 'natural' thing, including one's own mind, is subject to chance—that is, to necessity. That 'for nothing' is indeed the experienced correlate of the invisibility or non-representable blankness of the idea of Good itself."

10. *The Cloud of Unknowing*, trans. Clifton Walters (Baltimore: Penguin, 1961), pp. 90, 95.

11. Kierkegaard, S., *The Concept of Dread, op. cit.*, p. 111.

John Karefa-Smart

DOCTORS, DEVELOPMENT, AND DEMONS IN AFRICA

IT IS INTERESTING that only a few short years after the vociferous proclamation of the death of God, there are now lecture series, books and movies affirming that God's archenemy, the Devil, is alive, well, and active in all aspects of contemporary society. In this essay, I will deal with the demonic in terms of the problem of development as it affects my native continent of Africa.

I believe not in the Devil but in the reality of his existence. I have no certain knowledge that he exists as a person. I cannot give you an account of the way his kingdom is organized. I am not even sure that the Satan of the Hebrew and Greco-Roman tradition is the same as the *Krifi* of my own Temne tribe. All I can say is that I see a striking family resemblance; their works and influences seem the same. They seem to be at work wherever human beings are trying to fulfill the best that is in them, and wherever life is trying to keep death at bay. Of the universal reality of Evil, another synonym of the Devil, there is no doubt in my mind.

In your society and in mine I have seen Evil constantly battling against good. The hand of the demonic is seen in the wars, addictions, and crimes of our societies, as well as the political, economic, and social structures which we create to enslave our fellows and to perpetuate injustice.

Only a few years ago many of us in Africa, personally engaged in the struggle which eventually led to the end of colonial rule over the continent, would have scoffed at any suggestion that the Devil was not being completely routed from his hold on our countries. At the end of the Second World War, only Liberia, Egypt and Ethiopia and the minority-governed Union of South Africa were sovereign and independent states. A few years later Nwafor Orizu,

150

Namdi Azikiwe, and Kingsley Mbadiwe of Nigeria; Hastings Banda of Malawi; Aku Adjei, Suas Quartey and Koi Larbi of Ghana—among others—were inspired to leadership by ideas learned as students abroad. Kwame Nkrumah spearheaded the last wave of the attack against imperialism which had already started at the turn of the century and led his country to independence and to membership in the United Nations. By the end of 1959, Libya, Morocco, Tunisia, and Sudan had joined the ranks. Only one year later, in 1960, the independent African states numbered twenty-six. My own country, Sierra Leone, became independent in 1961 and the 100th member of the United Nations. In 1973 the only African countries that are not sovereign states are those still governed by Portugal; namely, Guinea-Bissau, Angola, and Mozambique; the small French enclave of Somalia; and the territory of Namibia, previously known as South West Africa. Rhodesia, under a regime controlled by a small white minority, has declared independence unilaterally, but is not recognized by most members of the U.N.

In country after country, however, the jubilation which came with independence has been replaced by the distress of internal strife. No less than thirteen states have succumbed to military rule, and in at least three others the leader is a virtual dictator. The reality of independence has turned out to be not quite so beneficial to all as was dreamed. Those of us who were motivated by the dream had not reckoned with the persistent power of the demonic. It would seem that ever since man was created in God's image, the Devil has striven to deface the image by encouraging man to exploit and enslave as many of his fellows as possible.

No African that I know doubts the reality of the Devil. Living as close to nature as we do, the Devil does not have as many technological devices to mask his presence as he does among you. However, in our preoccupation with development he has found a very useful disguise. This disguise is a false notion of development held out to us by powerful agents of his demonic power. These agents paint a picture which sets us apart from the rest of the world. One picture which we are encouraged to enter includes the rich, highly industrialized and technologically productive nations. Except for Japan, these are white nations. The other picture, which we are placed in, is that of the poor, predominantly agricultural, under-industrialized, illiterate, black nations. We are the "have-nots"—the others are the "haves." Their gross domestic products are impressively high, and their average per capita incomes are in the four or five figures. Whereas our gross domestic products are almost insignificant and our per capita average incomes are at the subsistence level, often less than 10 per cent of the poverty level of the "haves." They are the "developed" countries, so-called; we are the "underdeveloped." (Now after much embarrassed protest, chiefly at the United Nations, we are rather more nicely referred to as "developing" countries.)

In spite of this recent nicety, the Devil continues to artfully employ his technique of "divide and rule." Since the picture of the other camp is seen only in its glamour, we jealously grope after it, and devote more and more of our energies to "development." But this picture of development is a false picture. Its accumulated savings, huge sums of capital, and devotion to self-aggrandizement all mean exploiting others and denying them their basic human rights.

One of the demonic's favorite disguises here is the person of the successful Western business executive who derides and criticizes our concern for the well-being of the extended family and of the whole community. "You cannot make progress that way," he admonishes. "You must look after yourself, save, get rich, and invest your wealth. If you will give me exclusive right to exploit one or several of your natural resources, you and I will share the profits, and you will soon become rich. Your cities will have tall buildings, and your roads will be paved. Your shops will be full of the glamorous products of the factories of the West. Your leaders will ride in expensive cars. Your country will even show its flag on a prestigious national airline!" The Devil insists that the first step towards development is to learn that M-O-N-E-Y, whether it is pronounced dollar, pound, franc, mark, lira, or yen, buys everything.

Poor Devil! His victory would have been almost complete if we all would have fallen for this line. Almost two thousand years ago the same approach failed when he offered all the kingdoms of this world to a lonely and hungry searcher for the Truth in the deserts of Palestine. He was rebuffed then with an unexpected weapon— the truth that man does not live by bread alone. This weapon may yet save us in Africa. Modern incarnations of the devil are not eager for us to realize that development involves justice in society as much as it involves amelioration of physical deprivation. The hand that dangles the loaf of material affluence before our eyes must be firmly pushed aside so that we can see what weapon of further bondage is concealed in the other hand.

Another favorite disguise of the Devil is "power." As the dream which motivated early leaders in the struggle for independence begins to fade, it has not been an easy task to fulfill the expectations of the masses of the newly independent nations for a better life. This frustration has been the cue for the Devil to suggest to the leader or leaders: "You can achieve everything if only you have power. If you cannot get it at the polls, seize it. Eliminate the opposition, control the courts, remove hindrances to access to the national treasury, make alliances with the profit-hungry exploiters from abroad. There is nothing the masses like better than leaders with great power."

In country after country in Africa, leaders from the military and even a few civilian leaders have been enticed by this promise of power. These leaders have abolished constitutions, suspended parliaments, harassed and gagged opposition parties, and silenced courts under the unlimited powers of "state of emergency." There are now fewer than ten African nations where the people can freely choose their representatives in the legislature. Elsewhere, when they have a chance to choose at all, it is usually for a handpicked slate of candidates. Instead of being spokesmen for their constituencies, legislators are more often than not the henchmen for the party leader. What is deplorable is not that the multiparty parliamentary democracy that was inherited from colonial rule has been made a mockery. After all, this was foreign to the African understanding and could not survive in such different conditions. What is deplorable is the rise of a form of government designed only to increase the power and wealth of the leader and his party. This form of government assumes the character of the demonic.

This demonic quest for power disguises the fact that power corrupts and absolute power corrupts absolutely! In spite of all the concentration of power in the hands of the leader, the needs of the people remain unfulfilled. There is no amelioration of living conditions; food becomes scarce and expensive; unemployment increases; unattractive market prices discourage agriculture; access to education is available only to the children who share power; and nepotism more and more determines who shall enjoy the benefits of the state. Inevitably, almost as if at a signal from the Devil himself, who has now collected the soul of the leader as his due, the people react violently, the feet of clay crumble, and the leader is overthrown. *Sic transit gloria mundi.*

If the false picture of development so attractively portrayed by the Devil and his agents leads only to disaster, it is crucial that Africans seriously attempt to understand freedom and development constructively. True development is like the traditional African three-legged stool; it should rest firmly on an equal emphasis on economic growth, social justice, and self-dependence. An emphasis on one to the neglect of the others will lead to instability.

Social justice would ensure that the demonic temptation to concentrate wealth and power in the hands of the few could be resisted. There should be equitable distribution throughout the land of resources and the economic growth derived from them. The standard of living should rise equally for all individuals and sections of the nation. Appropriate institutions must be created to facilitate equitable distribution of each country's wealth. These institutions would provide for equitable ownership or tenure of land, equal access to education, and adequate health services for all. Self-dependence or self-reliance should be developed not for the purpose of a reactionary isolation but rather for essential development. All the external aid programmes of the first development decade of the U.N. failed to achieve their objective, I believe, because they resulted in an increased dependence on imported machinery, consumer goods, and technology. While such dependence increased, the benefactor countries benefited through international policies governing trade of raw materials and agricultural produce. The effect has been that the rich countries have gotten richer while the poor countries in comparison have become poorer. Policies which would encourage self-reliance depend on applying in international relations the same principle of social justice described as an essential leg to the stool of development.

The relationship between development and health also has certain demonic manifestations. Throughout Africa, tribal communities have for ages been engaged in a struggle against disease and death. They traditionally have regarded all forms of sickness as the result of forces of evil working against the individual or his family. Similarly, epidemics and plagues have been interpreted as the result of demonic forces at work against the community. It was possible to take individual or group action of a preventative nature to ward off the evil spirit or spirits with the help of powerful talismans (*sebe-s*), which were carried on the person, kept in the home, or posted at the entrance to the village. But an even more powerful weapon against any *Krifi* or *Gafei* was to obtain the help of a more powerful one. The tribes were wise enough to realize that the health of the community was not restricted to the physical state of the bodies of the members of the community. The health of the community was measured by indices which included the state of the weather, size of the harvest, prevalence of accidents (snake bites, injuries, deaths from lightning, etc.), the number of surviving infants, and other social and environmental conditions.

In each community there were certain persons skilled in discovering which particular malevolent spirit was the cause of a particular illness or pestilence, and who were able to prescribe the right potions or incantations to counter it. These persons were custodians of the health of the community. Although they perform what could be described as priestly functions, they more closely correspond to those persons in Western society called "doctors." Their business is to heal; to counter the methods through which the health of individuals and the community is jeopardized. In the final analysis, there is not all that much difference between the assumptions of the tribal custodians of health and those of their colleagues in the West. The bacteria and viruses of disease may be called little devils; physicians recognize them as powerful foes. The derangements of normal physiological functioning of the endocrine system, chemical imbalances which cause disease, are the scientific counterparts of the spirit of the Devil working within the human body.

The point is that in spite of the analysis of much human illness as psychosomatic, the end result—lack of well-being—is as real as any physical illness. The Devil and his agents are at work whether or not we have succeeded in finding out *how* they are at work. Similarly, the ills of our society—all those factors and conditions which imprison our spirits through fear, ignorance, and greed—are also real and are the work of the Devil. They hinder genuine growth and development, prevent the full blossoming of culture, and retard balanced progress toward maturity. The cure for this malaise or absence of well-being in individuals and in communities does not lie in setting up false gods. Even if it were true that what obtains in the industrialized countries is good for their citizens and communities, it is still not necessarily true that it is good for African countries. To blindly follow the example of the West would be to fall into the Devil's trap.

Nevertheless great strides have been made in Africa in the battle against disease. Beginning with the missionary physicians in the second half of the 19th century, later with colonial governments, and most recently with national governments, the major causes of physical illness and death have been attacked. The World Health Organization (WHO) with bilateral assistance from friendly governments has mounted campaigns against specific diseases on a wide front. Considerable success has been achieved against malaria, sleeping sickness, leprosy, smallpox and malnutrition.

Yet the same problems which "bedevil" economic and social development are also present in the health field. The temptation to gain riches and the absence of a system that would provide equitable health services to all have concentrated trained personnel and facilities in the cities and large urban communities. The majority of the people live in rural villages and farms and thus have only limited access to health services. This results in the further enrichment of the health professionals—notably physicians and pharmacists. Similarly, the almost complete dependence on foreign training, or on local institutions which are copies of foreign models, overtaxes the resources of the community. Dependence upon equipment and procedures which have little relevance to the most pressing local health problems prevents the development of self-reliance. The final tragedy is that considerable numbers of trained personnel either fail to return from training abroad, or else soon despair of practicing under conditions so greatly different from those in which they were trained. Therefore they make every effort to return to richer professional and economic satisfactions abroad. It would appear that demonic influences prevent as much as possible the necessary roles of doctors and health professionals in the process of development.

The significance of the vignettes I have portrayed is that development must be seen essentially as a progressive exorcism of the Devil from society. As long as the Devil is in control there can be no well-being in either the social or the physical environment. The true role of all who would be doctors or healers in the community is to cast out the Devil; and thereby to release the human spirit from bondage; to restore health; and to make true growth and development possible. All who participate in this exorcism are the true healers so urgently needed by the disabled and disadvantaged in Africa. To this saving group, whom I collectively label the "true doctors" of society, belong all who proclaim justice, fight against oppression, empower the powerless, develop self-reliance in the dependent, and refuse to sell their souls for money and power. Strong and crafty as the Devil may be, the promise of history is that he does not have the last word. Neither in Africa nor elsewhere in God's world will the final victory be his.

CONTRIBUTORS TO THIS COLLECTION

ANANDA COOMARASWAMY was born in Ceylon in 1877 and received his education at the University of London in the natural sciences. His international reputation, however, was achieved through prolific research and writing in the areas of comparative culture and religion. A Fellow for Research in Indian, Persian and Islamic Art at the Museum of Fine Arts in Boston, Mass., Coomaraswamy was also Keeper of the Indian Collection at the same institution for thirty years until his death in 1947. During this period, he developed the first and one of the most extensive Asian collections in the United States. A new edition of the scholarly works of Ananda Coomaraswamy is forthcoming from the Bollingen Foundation of Princeton, N.J.

RADU FLORESCU is Associate Professor of History at Boston College. In addition to being the author of many articles and books on Romanian and East European history, Professor Florescu has recently received notoriety for his best-selling works, *In Search of Dracula* and *Dracula: A Biography of Vlad the Impaler*, co-authored with Raymond T. McNally. He has appeared on numerous talk shows on television and lectured across the United States. Dr. Florescu's next book will explore the factual background of another Gothic literary legend, Mary Shelley's *Frankenstein*.

JOHN KAREFA-SMART is Visiting Professor of International Health at the Harvard School of Public Health. A distinguished physician, teacher, and diplomat, Dr. Karefa-Smart has held the post of Cabinet Minister in Sierra Leone and has served as Assistant Director of the World Health Organization, a specialized agency of the United Nations.

ERAZIM KOHÁK is Professor of Philosophy at Boston University. A noted philosopher and social phenomenologist, Professor Kohák's recently published books have included *Masaryk on Marx* and the highly

157

praised *The Victors and the Vanquished*, co-authored with Heda Kovaly. Soon to appear is a book on the philosophy of Edmund Husserl entitled, *The Project of Phenomenology in Ideen I*.

CARTER LINDBERG is Assistant Professor of Church History at Boston University School of Theology. A frequent contributor to journals in medieval and Reformation history, including *Lutherische Rundschau, Una Sancta* and *Sixteenth Century Journal*, Professor Lindberg's forthcoming translation of the works of *Karlstadt*, the German Protestant reformer, is being published by Brill, of the Netherlands, in its *Textus Minores* series.

ARTHUR McGILL is Professor of Theology at Harvard Divinity School. A frequent and well-known contributor to journals in theology and literature, Professor McGill's more recent books include: *The Celebration of Flesh: Poetry and the Christian Life*, and *The Many-Faced Argument*, co-edited with John Hick.

HERBERT MASON is University Professor of Religion and Islamic History at Boston University. A noted poet, translator and author, Professor Mason's more recent works include: *Reflections on the Middle-East Crisis, Two Statesmen of Medieval Islam*, and the award-winning *Gilgamesh: A Verse Narrative*. Soon to appear are *Hallaj: A Dramatic Narrative*, and a translation of *The Passion of al-Hallaj* (4 vols.) by Louis Massignon. Dr. Mason is also co-editor of *Humaniora Islamica: An Annual of Islamic Studies and the Humanities*.

JOHN R. MAY is Associate Professor of Religious Studies at Loyola University in New Orleans. Author of *Toward a New Earth: Apocalypse in the American Novel*, Fr. May has contributed regularly in recent years to literary and theological journals. An Associate Editor for Religion and Culture of *Horizons*, journal of the College Theology Society, he is presently completing a hermeneutical study of the fiction of Flannery O'Connor and collaborating with Ernest Ferlita on *Film Odyssey*, an analysis of the quest for meaning in recent cinema.

ALAN M. OLSON, editor of this collection, is Assistant Professor of Religion at Boston University, and a member of the Advisory Board of The Boston University Institute for Philosophy of Religion and Philosophical Theology. Forthcoming from Martinus Nijhoff (The Hague), is a book entitled: *Transcendence and the Spirit: An Interpretation of the Philosophy of Karl Jaspers*.

ANN BELFORD ULANOV is Professor of Religion and Psychiatry at Union Theological Seminary, New York City, and a psychotherapist in private practice. A noted contributor to journals of psychology, psychiatry and religion, Professor Ulanov's most recent work is entitled *The Feminine in Jungian Psychology and Christian Theology.*

E. V. WALTER is Simon Senior Research Fellow at the University of Manchester, England, on leave from his position as Professor of Sociology at Boston University, and from the Laboratory of Community Psychiatry, Harvard University, where he is a Research Associate. At present, Professor Walter is engaged in research on the history, ethnography and philosophy of social problems, and is writing a book on milieus of the poor. He is also exploring various dimensions of the quest for re-enchantment, and the histories of the boundaries between magic, religion and science. He is the author of *Terror and Resistance: A Study of Political Violence,* and has written numerous essays on various topics in the social sciences.